GOD AS
NOTHING.

GOD AS NOTHING.

GILBERT MÁRKUS

DARTON · LONGMAN + TODD
INTELLIGENT ◆ INSPIRATIONAL ◆ INCLUSIVE
SPIRITUAL BOOKS

In memoriam
Herberti McCabe O.P.
amici, fratris, doctoris

First published in 2025 by
Darton, Longman and Todd Ltd
Unit 1, The Exchange
6 Scarbrook Road
Croydon CR0 1UH
editorial@darton-longman-todd.co.uk

This product conforms to the requirements of the European Union's General Product Safety Regulations (GPSR).
EU Authorised Representative for GPSR:
Easy Access System Europe –
Mustamäe tee 50, 10621 Tallinn, Estonia
gpsr.requests@easproject.com

ISBN: 978-1-917362-04-7

Acknowledgements
The author is grateful to Carcanet Press for permission to reproduce poetry by Paul Celan, and to Bloodaxe Books and Orion Publishing Group for permission to reproduce poetry by R. S. Thomas.

A catalogue record for this book is available from the British Library.

Printed and bound in Great Britain by Short Run Press, Exeter

CONTENTS.

INTRODUCTION.

THIS BOOK HAS only one idea in it – or at least at the heart of it. It is not an easy idea to express or to understand, so we will approach it from various angles, circling it and poking it with various different sticks (biblical, historical, philosophical, poetic) to see what it is like and what it might mean. The idea is this: Christians (and Jews and Muslims) who believe in a Creator do so as a result of asking a natural question, 'Why does anything exist, rather than nothing?' This question underlies all our talk about God. And the answer to that question cannot be 'something which exists', because that would be one of the things we were seeking to explain. If God created everything that exists, God cannot be one of the things that exist. God is no thing. Or Nothing.

This is a difficult idea, and it is made more difficult by the fact that to talk about Creation we are forced to use language which constantly threatens to mislead us. Our language treats 'God' *grammatically* as if it were a personal name, and so believers assume that there must be an individual being to whom it corresponds. Believers say all kinds of things about God ('he' or 'she' is 'good' or 'strong' or 'merciful' or 'present') all of which make God *sound* like an individual being with certain characteristics. But that is simply because we have to express ourselves in ordinary human language which was created to talk about individual existing beings. And so, our language presents us with a picture which misleads us. We may be reminded of a remark by Wittgenstein: 'A picture held us captive. And we could not get outside it, for it lay in our language and language seemed to repeat it to us inexorably' (1958, §115).

7

The idea of God as Nothing is important because some believers (theists) and almost all atheists who fight each other over 'the question of God' treat their disagreement as being about some big, powerful, invisible person, an individual being, for whose existence there may or may not be evidence or arguments.

The purpose of this book is to show that this controversy between theists and atheists, which has heated up considerably in the last few years, is being conducted in misleading terms. The argument is conducted as if atheists believed in all the things that exist in the universe, and theists also believed in all those beings but also believed in one additional being which they call 'God'. But that is not what theists are committed to believing, and this mistake makes the entire debate rather sterile and pointless.

I am not suggesting that believers and atheists agree. Of course they disagree, but I will argue that what they disagree about is not whether there is a God. They disagree about whether it is meaningful to ask why the world exists, rather than nothing existing at all. They disagree about the meaningfulness of looking at the world, at everything that is, and seeing it as a mystery.

What I offer here is not a proof or an argument for or against the 'God hypothesis', but a pursuit of this one thought as it has appeared during the long and developing tradition of Jewish and Christian traditions. I trace it as a constant element in those traditions, though often somewhat disguised. As Wittgenstein remarked, 'How small a thought it takes to fill a whole life.' Well, if one small thought can fill a whole life, it can certainly fill a small book.

I hope that tracing this one thought through centuries of their tradition will be liberating for Christians (and for others who use the word 'God'); it may relieve them of some difficulties they have which arise from the language we use. And I hope it will also be illuminating for atheists to discover that the God that most of them don't believe in is the God that Christians don't believe in either.

Once we have grasped that thought, we will come to realise that what is diametrically opposed to faith is not atheism, as most modern commentators seem to assume, but idolatry. Worshipping something – anything at all that might or might not exist in the universe of existing beings, even if you call it 'God' – is idolatry. And it is idolatry that appears to be the opposite of faith in the Bible, not atheism.

There is not much that is very original in this book. Such pearls as there are have mostly been taken from other writers whom I hope I have acknowledged at the appropriate moments. My contribution has been largely to string the pearls together and to give a sense of the continuity of this one thought in the tradition, and to discuss it in language which I hope is as accessible and as natural as possible.

I am grateful to many teachers and students who have shaped my thinking, but I must mention four in particular – all Dominican friars of the English Province – whose work has inspired me more than most. Fergus Kerr and Gareth Moore introduced me to the thought of Wittgenstein in the 1980s – and the title of this book, *God as Nothing*, has been stolen (shamelessly) from Gareth's STL thesis in Oxford, a copy of which he gave me and which I have treasured ever since. For their radical reading of Thomas Aquinas which has also profoundly shaped my thinking, I am indebted to my inspirational teachers Brian Davies and, more than anyone, Herbert McCabe, to whose memory this book is dedicated.

CHAPTER ONE.

GENESIS AS PARODY IN THE ANCIENT NEAR EAST

HUMAN BEINGS TELL stories. Sometimes we do it simply to entertain each other, sometimes we do it for money, or in order to gain an advantage. But we also tell stories to explain the way things are, to orientate ourselves in a world which would otherwise seem chaotic and meaningless. Parents tell their children stories, at least in part, to help them grow in wisdom and understanding of the world. The Church also tells stories intended to nourish wisdom and understanding – stories of all sorts, which can be read in many different ways. Clearly many of the Church's stories are fictions: Jesus told parables about farmers and grapevines, fathers and sons, householders and burglars, landlords and tenants, virgins and oil-lamps. These were fictions designed to offer the hearer (or later the reader) a new way of seeing, to sow seeds of doubt among false certainties, and to offer different ways of imagining and living our lives. Jesus did not tell parables in order to give his hearers accurate information about grapes or lost sheep or tower-building, though those are the materials his stories use. He sought to provoke their imaginations and enable them to grasp his truth. If that is true of his parables, perhaps we should read other parts of the Bible like that as well.

The book of Genesis, for example, looks *on the surface* as if it should give us information about the beginnings of the universe and the origins of humanity. Indeed, some Christians do read it that way, and they conclude that the world is only a few thousand years old, that the theory of evolution is wrong (or even diabolical), and that fossils which scientists think are millions of years old are much more recent. But I suggest that to read Genesis like that is to misunderstand it. It is to mistake the appearance of the story (it *looks* like 'information') for its meaning. It is to confuse the practice of story-telling with the practice of the natural sciences, though these are actually different ways of talking, and different ways of expressing truth. The Genesis account of creation does offer us truth, precisely because it is *not* a scientifically accurate account of creation or any such thing. As Frederic Raphael once wittily said, 'Truth may be stranger than fiction, but fiction is truer.' In this first chapter we are going to look at the book of Genesis for the kind of truth it offers.

Genesis was written in its present form in the first millennium BC, but it was woven together out of much earlier strands of story-telling. So, before we look at the book of Genesis we are going to look back a thousand years earlier than that, to think about those earlier strands, stories written in Mesopotamia (a name which means 'between the rivers', the rivers in question being the Tigris and the Euphrates). In this region from about 3000 BC, people were reciting myths, sagas and poems, several of which have survived in whole or in part written on clay tablets in a script now known as cuneiform (literally 'wedge-shaped'). The earliest texts survive in a language called Sumerian, which as far as linguists can tell is not related to any other known language. Later, these stories were re-told in a language called Akkadian (after the city of Akkad), which is the earliest known semitic language.[1] The Sumerian kingdoms and Sumerian language disappeared as a result of the Akkadian takeover, but Sumerian stories survived by being absorbed into the new language; they were taken up and recycled in the Akkadian tongue from about 2000 BC onwards, being recited, recorded, and revised over and over again.

The surviving texts of these stories and poems suggest that there was never a single 'original version'. Rather there were many traditions circulating which crystallised in various ways at different times. There are huge quantities of this Akkadian material – there are around 130,000 tablets and fragments in the British Museum alone, not to mention those lying in other museum store-rooms still waiting to be read – but I will highlight only a few themes from a handful of texts before discussing their relationship to the Jewish and Christian story found in the book of Genesis. In what follows I will be using the fine translation by Stephanie Dalley in *Myths from Mesopotamia*, which includes all the stories I will refer to and several others besides.

STORIES OF THE GODS: ATRAHASIS

The first story we will look is called *Atrahasis*. This is actually the name of a man, the central figure in the narrative, whose name means 'extra-wise' in Akkadian. As we shall see, the *Atrahasis* story lay behind the Hebrew Genesis story, but it did so in ways which demand a careful reading. It is the story of how gods shaped the world, how they brought about a flood to destroy humankind, and how the wise Atrahasis survived the flood and built a big boat, saving himself and lots of animals

---

[1]   No longer spoken, Akkadian is a broad term which embraces various dialects. The last known document written in Akkadian cuneiform script was made in the first century AD. Of course, though Akkadian is no longer spoken, Hebrew and Arabic are members of the same family of languages, and are spoken today by millions·

which he also took on board – is this beginning to sound a bit familiar?

There is plenty that is unfamiliar too. It starts off, for example, with a large number of gods. There are greater gods and lesser gods, older gods and younger gods. The older gods are earth gods, the *Anunnaki,* who will later become judges in the underworld. The older gods make a lot of younger gods, sky-gods called *Igigi,* and the reason for making them is interesting. The older *Anunnaki* make the *Igigi* because they themselves are getting tired. The *Anunnaki* inhabit the world where they work together, digging out canals, carving out the courses of rivers, building, and so on. They begin to tire of their labours, so they make sky gods, *Igigi,* to do the work for them. The work is hard, and it is worth noting that the work itself is basically 'landscape formation'. They are making a world, digging out the courses of the Tigris and Euphrates, the two mighty rivers which form the world of Mesopotamia in which these stories were written.

> *When the gods instead of man*
> *did the work, bore the loads,*
> *the gods' load was too great,*
> *the work too hard, the trouble too much.*
> *The great Anunnaki made the Igigi*
> *to carry the workload sevenfold.*
> *... The gods had to dig out canals,*
> *had to clear channels, the lifelines of the land,*
> *the Igigi had to dig out canals ....*
> *the gods dug out the Tigris river,*
> *and then dug out the Euphrates ...*
> *For 3,600 years they bore the excess,*
> *hard work, night and day.*
> *They groaned and blamed each other,*
> *grumbled over the masses of excavated soil:*
> *'Let us confront our ... chamberlain,*
> *and get him to relieve us of our hard work!'*

Then [ ] made his voice heard,
and spoke to the gods as his brothers:
'Come, let us carry the counsellor of the gods,
the warrior, from his dwelling ...
Now cry battle! Let us mix fight with battle!'
The gods listened to his speech, set fire to their tools,
put aside their spades for fire,
their loads for the fire-god,
they flared up. When they reached
the gate of Ellil's[2] warrior dwelling
it was night.

These may be gods, but they live in a world of class struggle, of slavery and tyranny, and of resistance – a world which closely resembles the human world of the ancient near east. This army of overworked gods besieges Ellil's house, getting him out of his bed. Ellil has his weapons brought to him, but tells his divine attendants to stand at their posts. Various other gods are summoned to help him. He sends one to find out what the *Igigi* are complaining about. They answer:

'Every single one of us gods has declared war!
We have put a stop to the digging.
The load is excessive. It is killing us.
Our work is too hard, the trouble too much.
So every single one of us gods
has agreed to complain to Ellil.'

The assembled Anunnaki consult among themselves and are sympathetic to the complaint of the Igigi: 'Why are we blaming them? Their work was too hard ...' Eventually a solution is found when one of the Anunnaki speaks:

---

[2] His name is Enlil in Sumerian. A god whose nature and attributes are still uncertain, but he is head of the younger generation of Sumerian and Akkadian (sky-)gods. His cult centre is at Nippur. His temple called Ekur.

'Belet-ili, the womb-goddess, is present.
Let the womb-goddess create offspring,
and let man bear the load of the gods!'
They called up the goddess
... to be creator of mankind.
'Create a mortal, that he may bear the yoke!
Let him bear the yoke, the work of Ellil,
let man bear the load of the gods.'

There is some difficulty about this proposal. Nintu (another name for the womb-goddess[3]) is reluctant to get involved in the process of generation, as it seems there is a danger of incurring ritual impurity. In the end she agrees to do it as long as Enki, who makes everything pure, is prepared to give her the clay. Enki agrees to the purification, and describes the process by which the man will be made. It involves the sacrifice of one of the gods, and the use of his flesh and blood to make the man:

'One god shall be slaughtered,
and the gods can be purified by immersion.
Nintu shall mix clay with his flesh and blood.
Then a god and a man will be mixed together in clay.'

The senior gods assent to the killing, and rituals of purification. Then:

In their assembly, they slaughtered Geshtu-e,
a god who had intelligence.
Nintu mixed clay with his flesh and blood.
... After she had mixed that clay,
she called up the Anunnaki, the great gods.
The Igigi, the great gods,
spat spittle upon the clay.

---

[3] The name means 'birth-lady'.

16

The combination of a god's flesh and blood, the clay of the earth and spittle of the gods points towards something unique about the man, perhaps something 'divine'. He is a compound of earthinesss and divinity. The other gods thank Nintu and praise her, for she has freed them from their labours by producing a human slave to do their work for them. She goes on to make more people, seven men and seven women, out of clay, and so the whole story of human fertility begins.

Now the gods have made mankind to serve them as slaves, but they are troublesome and noisy slaves. The fertility of the seven men and seven women has brought problems:

> Six hundred years passed,
> and the country became too wide, the people too numerous.
> The country was as noisy as a bellowing bull.
> The god grew restless at their racket,
> Ellil had to listen to their noise.
> He addressed the great gods:
> 'The noise of mankind has become too much ...
> give the order that šuruppu-disease shall break out.'

And so the gods agree to send a dreadful plague on humanity, to be delivered by the god Namtara. But among the gods there is one called Enki who acts almost like a secret agent or spy on behalf of humanity. After appalling suffering among the humans, Enki tells Atrahasis how to bring the famine to an end by leading his people in a kind of strike against the gods. Instead of revering their usual gods and goddesses, they build a temple and offer bread to Namtara, the disease-bringer, who takes away his plague of šuruppu. Things become quiet for another six hundred years, but then the noise of humanity begins to trouble the gods again, so another curse falls on humanity: drought and famine, this time brought by a god called Adad. But, once again, building a temple to Adad and making offerings to him moves him to lift the curse of drought

17

and famine. And six hundred years later another such disaster falls on the people – drought, disease, and famine leading to cannibalism – alleviated in the same way. Eventually the gods decide to send a flood to wipe out humanity and its noise, but the philanthropic god Enki once again secretly reveals their plan to his servant Atrahasis, warning him to prepare himself:

> 'Dismantle the house, build a boat,
> reject possessions, and save living things.
> The boat that you build ...
> roof it like the Apsu,[4] so that the Sun cannot see inside it.'

Atrahasis rescues animals: pure ones, fat ones, those that fly, cattle of Shakan, wild animals of the open country, are all taken on board together with his family. Then:

> The Flood roared like a bull,
> like a wild ass screaming the winds howled.
> The darkness was total, there was no sun.

Many of the gods become in turn depressed and horrified; they wail in grief as drowned bodies 'clog the river like dragonflies', but though they weep and bleat they are impotent to act as the flood's destruction advances. Then the god Ellil notices Atrahasis's boat, and is furious with Enki and the Igigi, who have subverted the murderous will of the Anunnaki.

> 'We, the great Anunna, all of us,
> agreed together on oath!
> No form of life should have escaped.
> How did any man survive the catastrophe?'

---

[4] Apsu is the realm of fresh water beneath the earth (compare Genesis 1 and its water above and below the earth). As it is underground, clearly the sun cannot 'see' inside that realm, just as the gods cannot see inside Atrahasis's boat.

Anu made his voice heard
and spoke to the warrior Ellil,
'Who but Enki would do this?'
... Enki spoke and made his voice heard
and spoke to the great gods,
'I did it in defiance of you!
I made sure life was preserved.'

The last part of *Atrahasis* is rather fragmentary, but it seems that the gods find other ways of controlling human fertility so that the population should no longer increase so noisily, disturbing the gods' peace and quiet. They have various methods of population-control: causing stillbirths, sending demons who 'snatch a baby from its mother's lap' (possibly some fatal disease, or maybe child sacrifice?) and the establishment of a class of women with cultic roles who are forbidden to bear children. So at last there is some restraint on the multiplication of humanity and its expansion throughout the earth. The gods will no longer suffer from excessive human noise or feel threatened by the swarming crowds of a fecund and constantly proliferating humanity.

STORIES OF THE GODS: GILGAMESH

Let us now leave *Atrahasis* to look at another Mesopotamian myth, the *Epic of Gilgamesh*, which is the longest surviving Akkadian text of this type. It tells the saga of a great man called Gilgamesh, and uses his story to explore themes of violence, sex, friendship and – above all – death and immortality. The story as we now have it contains elements of several earlier independent folk tales which were woven together, and the whole work was constantly altered over many centuries.

There is some evidence that Gilgamesh was remembered as a Sumerian king of Uruk, or the son of a Sumerian king. One version of the tale says that his father was a *lillu*, a man with demonic qualities, and high priest of Kullab in the kingdom of Uruk. But his mother is divine – Ninsun, the Wild Cow goddess – and so he himself is partly divine, inheriting a two-thirds share of her divinity, as a result of which his name appears in lists of the gods. The *Epic of Gilgamesh* opens with praise of the great hero, and tells of his ancestry, human and divine:

> *A hero born of Uruk, a goring wild bull.*
> *He marches at the front as leader,*
> *he goes behind as the support of his brothers,*
> *a strong net, the protection of his men ...*
> *Son of Lugalbanda, Gilgamesh, perfect in strength,*
> *Son of the lofty cow, the wild cow Ninsun.*
> *He is Gilgamesh, perfect in splendour,*
> *who opened up passes in the mountains,*
> *who could dig pits even in the mountainside,*
> *who crossed the ocean, the broad seas, as far as the sunrise.*
> *Who inspected the edges of the world, kept searching*
>   *for eternal life.*
> *... Two thirds of him was divine, and one third mortal.*

But this magnificent and powerful character misuses his macho talents. He dominates all the young men of Uruk, and will not leave their brides and young women alone. They complain to the gods, and the goddess Aruru creates an opponent for Gilgamesh, someone who can resist him. This is Enkidu, a wild and shaggy man, 'dressed as cattle are' (i.e. presumably, not dressed at all except in his own hair), living wild on the mountains, eating vegetation and drinking water with other animals. Apparently the intention is that by creating such a powerful wild man the gods can restrain the otherwise unequalled power of Gilgamesh. Enkidu is truly wild, knowing 'neither people nor country'. He lives with the animals and like the animals, and because his loyalty is to the animal kingdom, not to humanity, he helps animals to escape from traps laid by hunters. So the hunters seek the advice of Gilgamesh who knows exactly what to do to 'tame' this wild Enkidu, and he advises one of the hunters how to accomplish it. A prostitute, Shamhat, must be brought by one of the hunters to tempt Gilgamesh:

> 'When [Enkidu] approaches the cattle at the watering place,
> [Shamhat] must take off her clothes and reveal her
>   attractions.
> He will see her and go to her.
> Then his cattle, who have grown up in open country with
>   him,
> will become alien to him.'

And so it is done. Gilgamesh comes to the water to drink like all the other wild animals, while Shamhat and the hunter lie in wait. The hunter tells her:

> 'Here he is Shamhat, bare your bosom,
> open your legs and reveal your attractions.
> ... Spread open your garments, and let him lie upon you.
> Do for him, the primitive man, as women do ...'
> For six days and seven nights Enkidu was aroused
> and poured himself into Shamhat ...

After it is all over, 'when he was sated with her charms', Enkidu has changed. He has become human, estranged from the animals:

> The gazelles saw Enkidu and scattered,
> the cattle of the open country kept away from his body.
> For Enkidu had stripped (?), his body was too clean.
> ... Enkidu had been diminished, he could not run as
>   before.
> Yet he had acquired judgement, had become wiser.

Through his union with Shamhat, Enkidu has been transformed – from hairy to clean, from wild to civilised, from solitary to social – and now sits at Shamhat's feet and converses with her, and she tell him of the consequence of his union with her: 'You have become profound, like a god.' She guides him to Uruk, where he meets and fights with Gilgamesh, but then becomes his friend. Together Enkidu and Gilgamesh enjoy several heroic adventures, eventually going into a pine forest to find Humbaba the Intestine-Faced:

> *whose shout is the Flood weapon,*
> *whose utterance is Fire,*
> *and whose breath is Death,*
> *who can hear for a distance of sixty leagues through the*
> *   forest –*
> *so who can penetrate his forest?*

Enkidu and Gilgamesh kill Humbaba, and move on. The goddess Ishtar woos Gilgamesh, but he refuses her advances. She seeks revenge then, going to her father, Anu, and obtaining from him the Bull of Heaven – a kind of divine monster – with which she intends to destroy Gilgamesh. But Enkidu and Gilgamesh slay the Bull of Heaven. With two of their mightiest monsters slain, the gods are now anxious about the power of the two friends; they decide one of them must die, and Enkidu is chosen. The death of Enkidu gives rise to much questioning about mortality. Perhaps the horror of death will be reduced by subsequent honour and fame, and by the love and grief of your friends, and the weeping of nature itself? After Enkidu's death, Gilgamesh wonders about his own mortality, if there is any way to avoid death: 'My friend whom I love has turned to clay. Am I not like him? Must I lie down too, never to rise again?' A long quest in search of the secret of immortality leads him to Ut-napishtim, who reminds him that he is mortal, but also gives him hope:

'Since the gods made you from the flesh of gods and of
mankind,
since the gods made you like your father and mother,
death is inevitable at some time, both for Gilgamesh and for
a fool,
but a throne is set down for you in the (divine) assembly ... '

Ut-napishtim also tells Gilgamesh a version of the flood story –
similar to the story in *Atrahasis*, except that in this version the
name of the man who has survived the flood in a boat is not
Atrahasis, but Up-napishtim himself:

'On the first day the tempest rose,
blew swiftly and brought the flood-weapon,
like a battle-force, the destructive kasusu–weapon passed
over the people.
No man could see his fellow,
nor could people be distinguished from the sky.
Even the gods were afraid of the flood-weapon.
They withdrew; they went up to the heaven of Anu.
The gods cowered, like dogs crouched by an outside wall.
Ishtar screamed like a woman giving birth;
the mistress of the gods was wailing ...
... The gods of the Anunnaki were weeping with her.
The gods, humbled, sat there weeping.
Their lips were closed and covered with scab.'

The boat eventually lands on mount Nimush as the waters
subside, and Up-napishtim says:

'When the seventh day arrived
I put out and released a dove.
The dove went; it came back ...
I put out and released released a swallow.
The swallow went; it came back.

23

... I put out and released a raven.
The raven went and saw the waters receding.
It ate, preened, lifted its tail, and did not turn round.
Then ... I made a sacrifice.
... the gods smelt the fragrance,
the gods gathered like flies over the sacrifice.'

One god, however, is excluded from the offering: Ellil, who had caused the terrible flood without consulting the other gods properly, gets nothing. Furthermore he is furious that any man has survived his flood. And not only has Ut-naptishtim survived, but after the flood he and his wife are blessed and become immortal: 'Henceforth Ut-naptishtim and his woman shall be as we gods are.' We have seen two Akkadian versions of the flood story, then. In *Atrahasis* the flood was part of the gods' attempt to solve the problem of human overpopulation; in *Gilgamesh* it seems to have another purpose, perhaps offering some kind of answer to the hero's questions about death and immortality.

GENESIS AND MESOPOTAMIAN MYTHS

Those Akkadian myths are exciting literature, compelling stories whose language and poetry come across powerfully even in modern English translation. These stories were circulating all over the Near East at the time when Hebrew writers were putting together their own ideas which would eventually form the book of Genesis. Akkadian myths provided a kind of quarry for stories and imagery which the authors of Genesis used to write their own account. We can see it in the story of the flood, for example. In Mesopotamian myth the gods seek to destroy humankind, but one man is forewarned by one of the gods and told to build an ark. He takes on board his family and also many animals (some versions say he took them on in pairs, two-by-two); all of them survived the flood, and finally the man sends out a succession of birds in order to find out whether dry land has appeared. To thank the gods for his survival he comes out of his ark and offers sacrifice: 'the gods smelt the pleasant fragrance, and gathered over the sacrifice like flies.' In Genesis (6:11-8:22) it is God who brings the flood, and he himself warns Noah to build the ark and to take his family and pairs of animals on board. Again, the occupants of the ark survive, and Noah sends out birds to find out if there is dry land. On leaving the ark he builds an altar and offers a sacrifice of animals, and 'the Lord smelled the pleasing odour'.

The story of the creation of mankind is described in *Atrahasis*: where the womb-goddess made a man of clay from the earth, mixed it with the flesh and blood of a sacrificed god, and then the other gods spat into the clay. In Genesis God 'formed man from the dust of the ground, and breathed into his nostrils the breath of life; and man became a living being.' The parallels – as well as the differences – are striking. In the creation story in Genesis, God's work of the second day involves separation:

> And God said, 'Let there be a firmament in the midst of the waters, and let it separate the waters from the waters.' And God made the firmament, and separated the waters which were under the firmament from the waters which were above the firmament. And it was so. And God called the firmament Heaven. And there was evening and there was morning a second day (1:6-8).

These two bodies of water, separated by the firmament of heaven, echo the traditional Mesopotamian cosmology in which the world has its origin in the mating of two deities, Tiamat, the 'sea goddess' whose realm is salt water and who represents chaos, and Apsu, the god of fresh water which is beneath the earth. In the Mesopotamian world-creation story a god called Marduk slays Tiamat and splits her body in half:

He sliced her in half like a fish for drying;
half of her he put up to roof the sky,
drew a bolt across and made a guard hold it.
Her waters he arranged so that they could not escape.

So again, we have waters above and waters below, constrained in their proper places by the separating action of a god, showing a correspondence between the cosmology of Mesopotamia and the later writings of Hebrew scripture.

GENESIS AS PARODY

The first translations of this Mesopotamian mythology into English were undertaken in London, in the British Museum. In 1872 an Assyriologist called George Smith was working on a tablet that recorded the Flood story. As he read, he was so excited that, according to a contemporary, '[He] jumped up and rushed about the room in a great state of excitement, and, to the astonishment of those present, began to undress himself.' Smith's excitement is understandable. He had not only discovered an interesting ancient text; he had discovered a story much older than the Bible which contained parallels to the Biblical text, suggesting that the authors of Genesis had drawn material from the mythologies of their 'pagan' neighbours. What did this mean for Christians (and for that matter Jews) and for their sense of the 'truth' of the Bible? In what sense could Genesis be the word of God? Only twelve years earlier Charles Darwin had published his essay *On the Origin of Species by Means of Natural Selection*, which would make it impossible for any scientifically literate person to accept Genesis as a literal description of creation. Now Smith's deciphering of cuneiform tablets showed that some aspects of Genesis were derivative, ancient reformulations of even earlier myths found among Israel's neighbours. This was just as shocking. How could the Jews and Christians believe that their account of creation was 'true' when it was so clearly dependent on other myths which they regarded as false? Were the first readers of Genesis so gullible that they didn't realise that it was simply a variation on the theme of a long-standing Middle-Eastern legend? Some have indeed assumed that this was evidence of their gullibility or their ignorance. It has been suggested that the authors of Genesis were tricksters, but we clever modern people have found them out; we have 'discovered' the dependence of Genesis on earlier myths, and we have gloriously debunked the Hebrew creation story.

But what this self-congratulatory view fails to understand is the intelligence and intentions of the Hebrew writers and their readers. If we focus merely on the fact that there are traces of Mesopotamian stories in Genesis, then we have misunderstood the text. The point is to ask what Israel *does* with those motifs. It will help if we think of Genesis as a deliberate parody – parody in the sense given by Linda Hutcheon who defines it as 'repetition with critical difference', a kind of joke with serious intent. Genesis parodies the Mesopotamian myths by recycling several of their themes, but doing so in ways which subvert the world-view of the Mesopotamian source-texts. We have looked at some of those Mesopotamian motifs. Anyone familiar with Genesis will have recognised them – and if you are not familiar, why not go off and read Genesis for half an hour and then come back here? Now we will consider some of the differences between the Mesopotamian and the Hebrew stories. It is precisely in the *differences* that we should be looking for the intent of the authors, or the 'truth' which Genesis offers to its readers. Because far from being unaware that Genesis was recycling Akkadian mythologies, the community which created Genesis can be presumed to have been consciously working on those stories, exploiting them, parodying them to create their own myth, the myth of monotheism and of the doctrine of Creation. And of course we cannot understand the parody, we do not 'get the joke', unless we understand what is being parodied and where the critical difference lies.

1. The most obvious difference is numerical: the Mesopotamians have many gods, while the Hebrew story has one. The difference is that between polytheism and monotheism, if you like.

2. But the difference is not merely numerical. The Mesopotamian gods are born, they have sex, they die. They have biographies, relationships, personalities. Things happen to them – they get annoyed by the noise of humans. They can be tricked. None of them is omnipotent. Each each of them may be powerful in some way, but none is omnipotent in the sense that everything depends on his or her will. They have to negotiate with each other, argue, and so on. This doesn't happen in Genesis. In Genesis there is just God, and he is the creator. Nothing happens to him. He doesn't *have* a story; he simply *makes* a story, the story of the world, and of the first creatures. He is not involved in the story as a participant. He doesn't negotiate. There is no one else 'there' to negotiate with. Nothing happens to him.

3. We can observe a kind of neediness among the Mesopotamian gods. The Anannuki are tired and need a rest, so they create the Igigi. The Igigi need a rest, so they create human beings to do the work. Clearly the gods are subject to the same kinds of stresses and strains as the mortals they create – mortals who are effectively created as slaves, as labouring bodies who will do the work that the gods would otherwise have to do. But in Genesis God seems to have no motive at all for creating Adam. God needs nothing. Why does he create Adam? There is no hint of a reason. There is no suggestion that Adam or his descendants will be slaves. Israel indeed had a strongly developed sense that God had *freed* them from slavery – so they would hardly tell stories in which the whole of humanity was created for slave labour. The God of Genesis appears to need nothing; his creation is gratuitous.

4. In the Mesopotamian stories, the world is created out of things which already exist – Marduk kills Tiamat, and dismembers her body to make the world, putting half of her up in the sky and leaving the rest of her in the deep. He makes rivers come out of her eyes. In other words the world's features are made out of the dismembered corpse of the goddess. Other gods exhaust themselves by digging the landscape to form rivers and mountains. In the book of Genesis, by contrast, God simply speaks and the cosmos comes into existence. He doesn't make the universe by re-arranging already existing stuff. 'In the beginning God created the heavens and the earth' – everything that is – and then he says simply, 'Let there be light', and there was light. 'Let this happen', and it happens. As the Psalmist says: 'He spoke, and it came to be; he commanded, it sprang into being' (33:9). This critical difference from the Mesopotamian myths underlies what has become in Jewish and Christian thought the idea of *creatio ex nihilo*, 'creation out of nothing'. It is a radical departure from other cosmogenic (world-making) myths.

5. In the Mesopotamian stories, the gods occupy space. They come and go to various places, surround each other, visit each other, get up and go to bed, and so on. And just as they occupy various positions in space they also dwell in time. So gods can do something for a specified period of time, like the Igigi digging and working for 3,600 years, before protesting, or like Marduk who falls asleep for seven nights. These gods are part of this world. They are beings like us, occupying time and space, albeit with powers that distinguish them from human beings. Again the God of Genesis chapter 1 is different. Rather than acting *in* time, as the gods do, he creates time. He separates light from dark, creating day and night, which are time (1:3-5). He creates the lights of the firmament 'to separate the day from the night', and has them 'for signs and for seasons,

for days and years' (1:14-15). Although there are six days of creation, followed by a day in which God 'rests' from creation, they are days which he himself has created. God himself does not seem to occupy time or space, for time and space are dimensions of the created world, and God is the reason that time and space exist at all.[5] He himself is therefore beyond time and space. He has no past, present or future. He cannot be here or there. Unlike the Mesopotamian gods, he has no history. He simply makes history, and therefore cannot be part of it. In Genesis there is no time or space until God starts creating it. There is a beginning, when God makes things, but 'before' the beginning there is nothing,[6] or there is just God – which is more or less the same thing, if 'God is nothing'.[7]

6.   Another way of making this same point, more or less, is to say that in Mesopotamian belief there is continuity between the gods and humanity; the gods share a space with human beings. In general the Genesis parody

---

[5]   In the second and third chapters of Genesis we encounter a more anthropomorphic view of God: 'They heard the sound of the Lord God walking in the garden', for example (2: 8), but this is a different story working in a different way. We are concerned with the dynamic of the first chapter for the present.

[6]   'Before' is in quotes here because, obviously, nothing can be 'before' time. 'Before' and 'after' are only conceivable *within* time.

[7]   The statement that God 'ceased from working' or 'rested' on the seventh day is not traditionally understood as indicating that God spent six of *his* days working and then rested on *his* seventh day; it is rather that there were six 'days' of creation, and thereafter creation ceased in *its* seventh day. Nevertheless it is interesting that in Genesis 2:2 God 'rested' (*shabbat*) on the day immediately following the creation of Adam. Is this an echo of the Akkadian story of the creation of humanity in which the gods create man to do their work for them, that is to say, to give them a rest? If so, the story here is also a subversion of the Akkadian myth, for in that story the gods *need* a rest, being tired, and so they create man to work for them, meaning that they *need* man. Here in Genesis 2, however, there is no sense that God needs a rest, nor that Adam should be working for God. Indeed, there is no work envisaged for Adam in God's initial creation. Is this another parody of the Mesopotamian story, for different purposes?

removes such continuity. There is an absolute difference between the Creator and his creation.

7. Some other details of the Hebrew text of Genesis are interesting and perhaps revealing of the parody intended by the writers. Where Genesis says there was 'darkness on the face of the deep' the word for 'deep' is *tihom*, a word which echoes the related name of the goddess Tiamat in Mesopotamia. But where the Mesopotamian epic has Tiamat as a mother goddess, a creature of chaos and rebellion, personifying the chaotic and destructive power of the sea, for Genesis the *tihom* is completely depersonalised, with no power of its own. It's just 'the deep'.

8. Another Mesopotamian god's name is carefully avoided by the writer of Genesis. In the story of the wild man Enkidu he was 'civilised' by having sex with Shamhat. She was a temple prostitute dedicated to the god Shamash, the Akkadian sun god – his name simply means 'sun'. Perhaps that is why in Genesis, when God creates the sun and the moon, the author deliberately avoids mentioning the sun by name. The Hebrew name for the sun is *shemesh*, obviously related to the name of the Akkadian sun-god, Shamash; but the author of Genesis carefully describes the sun as 'the greater light' without using the Hebrew word for the sun. He won't use the word *shemesh*, perhaps to avoid giving the impression that God has created another god, a sun-god.

9. We might also note something about the Hebrew word *bara'* 'he made' – the second word in the whole book of Genesis. This word is only ever used when God is its subject. It is a word for what God does when he creates, and for absolutely nothing else (though other Hebrew verbs may be used for God's creating). We talk equivocally in English about God making things, and people making things. We talk about God as the creator of the world, but

also about Shostakovich as the creator of string quartets. We don't have a word, as Hebrew does, which refers solely to God's activity. In Hebrew the word *bara'* is only ever used of God's creative act. Perhaps the implication is that divine making is not like human making. We make things out of other things, as the Mesopotamian gods did using clay, blood and so on. But the God of the Genesis parody makes everything out of nothing. When we make something we are limited by the material we are using; there are no such limits on God's activity, for he simply 'speaks' and it comes to be. It exists because that is his will.

10. Akkadian myth attributes the flooding of the world to the gods being disturbed by humanity. Ellil says, 'The noise of mankind has become too much, and I am losing sleep over their racket'. But the Genesis parody moralises the flood story, so that it is no longer about the impact of humanity on the gods or God; it is now about morality. God says, 'I have determined to make an end of all flesh, for the earth is filled with violence through them.' Discussion of God turns not to what God is like, or what he needs, but to discussion of humans as ethical creatures.

My argument here is that Genesis is, at least in part, a witty parody of Mesopotamian myths, and that the purpose of the parody is to highlight critical differences between the Mesopotamian notion of gods and the Biblical notion of God. When Christians call Genesis 'the Word of God' we are asserting that by reading it we come to the truth. But 'the truth' in this sense does not mean 'accurate and detailed scientific information about the origin of the world'. It means 'the truth that sets you free' (John 8:32) – and whatever the pros and cons of fossil evidence, the theory of evolution, or the geological evidence of the age of the earth, they do not in themselves offer the kind of freedom that Jesus was talking about when he said that. The truth of the Genesis-parody is that there are no gods; there is only God, who is not one of the gods, or one of anything.

It may be worth conducting a little thought-experiment to illustrate this point. If you believe in hundreds of gods like the Akkadians, you are clearly a polytheist. If you believe in ten gods you are still a polytheist, you just believe in a smaller number of the same kind of thing. If you believe in ten gods, and nine of those gods kill and eat the tenth one, they are still the same kind of gods, but you have slightly fewer. Now there are only nine of them left.

But what if, rather than nine gods killing the tenth, one of those ten gods managed to kill and eat the other nine? Then there would be only one god left standing. If you believed in this one god, the survivor who had slain his kin, would that make you a monotheist? In a very superficial sense it might do: you only believe in one of these supernatural beings now. But the one being you believe in is still in principle the same kind of being as the nine he has killed, the kind of being the Akkadians imagined: a being capable of being killed, of having a story, of sharing a common space with another being, and therefore of existing within a universe. In a sense you could say you were now a polytheist with only one god. Our comparison between Mesopotamian and Israelite stories shows that the Hebrews have invented a more radical kind of monotheism. They are inventing a world where there are no gods, a world which is simply created by God. They have invented an idea of God which is such that there never *could* be two of them – not because there just *happens* to be only one, but because 'God' is not the name of any existing thing in the universe. He is not any kind of thing, because he is the creator of every thing.

From our reading of Genesis as parody, we can perhaps adopt a few pithy – if perhaps slightly puzzling – expressions about the use of the word 'God' to help us orientate ourselves. Such expressions as these will keep cropping up in the following chapters.

- If everything-which-exists is created by God, then God cannot be one of the things which exist; we might therefore call him 'Nothing'.
- A complete description of the universe and of everything in it would not be incomplete if it lacked the word 'God'.
- If God is Creator, he creates time and space, and therefore is outside time and space.
- If God is outside time and space, he cannot change, for change is only possible in the world of 'before' and 'after'. Nor can he remain unchanged for any period of time, for that is also only possible for things which exist *within* time.
- Nothing can happen *to* God, because he is the source or origin of everything that happens.
- We use the word 'god' to describe beings whose stories are told in Mesopotamian myths (and many other myths throughout the world), and we use the word 'God' to name the Creator, who has no story at all. This can be quite misleading, because one word ('god') is a common noun referring to a kind of being, the other ('God') is a name we use to refer to a mystery which is not any kind of being at all but rather the cause of all being.

OTHER PICTURES OF GOD

This chapter has argued that Israel used materials drawn from the myths of neighbouring nations to create a radically new belief in Creation. That is not to say that there aren't other beliefs lurking around in the Hebrew Bible. There are plenty of images of God, and ways of talking about God, which speak of him as an individual being.

There are even traces of an earlier period of polytheism in the Bible too. Think of Psalm 82:

God has taken his place in the divine council;
in the midst of the gods he gives judgement:

34

'How long will you judge unjustly
and show partiality to the wicked?
Give justice to the weak and the fatherless;
maintain the right of the afflicted and the destitute.
Rescue the weak and the needy;
deliver them from the hand of the wicked.'
... I say 'You are gods,
sons of the Most High, all of you;
yet you shall die like men,
and fall like any prince.'

Here we have a survival of a picture where God 'the Most High' is surrounded by an assembly of minor gods (perhaps his sons), very like Ellil in Akkadian literature. A similar picture emerges from other biblical texts such as Psalm 95:3:[8]

For the Lord is a great God,
a great king above all gods.

I am not arguing, therefore, that ancient Israel had a uniform and radical monotheism from the beginning, nor that this theological idea was consistently promoted in all her writings over the centuries. It does seem, however, that the authors of parts of Genesis promoted a new and radical monotheism by parodying Akkadian myths, and that this was an adventure in thinking which emerged from an earlier tradition in which the god of Israel was merely one of the gods of the nations. The rest of this book will pursue this shocking discovery that believing in God actually frees us from believing in gods – not 'other gods', but *any* gods.

[8]   See also for example Exodus 15:11; Psalm 29:1; 89:7; Job 38:4-7.

CHAPTER TWO.

GOD'S NAME AND GOD'S JUSTICE

IN THE FIRST chapter we looked at how the authors of parts of Genesis used stories about creation, the foundation of the world, to express a new insight that everything which exists is created. Israel 'squeezed the gods out of the world'. None of the things which exist is God, because God is the cause of existence. No individual being can be identified as God, because God is the creator of all beings, and therefore cannot be listed among the things which merely are. This is one of the roots of the Jewish and Christian idea of 'God as Nothing'.

Of course, there are lots of places in the Hebrew Bible where the idea of radical monotheism, and therefore the idea of 'God as Nothing', is apparently called into question. As we saw in the last chapter, there are places where God, the God of Israel, seems to be one of several gods – the gods of the nations – in passages which have perhaps survived from a time before Israel developed its radical idea, or when it was still in doubt. There are also stories and images of God which suggest very much that he *is* one of the things that is around, and some Hebrew writers may very well even have thought of God as having something like a human body. They certainly wrote things that suggest this. When the

Bible says that God sees something, are we to understand that literally – that he has eyes? The Bible says that God is 'slow to anger', but this actually translates a Hebrew phrase which means 'long of nostril' (Exodus 36:6). We are told that God has a 'mighty hand and an outstretched arm' (Deuteronomy 4: 34), and that 'smoke went up from his nostrils and devouring fire from his mouth ... thick darkness under his feet' (Psalm 18:8-9). Are we supposed to take every image of God in the Hebrew Bible as a literal description of a physical being? Or perhaps we should imagine that the Hebrews were quite capable of speaking metaphorically about God, using the image of body-parts to express other ideas about God.

Having looked at the creation story of Genesis in the last chapter, we will now look at other passages in the Hebrew Bible which point towards the idea that God is not any kind of thing – not even an invisible and disembodied thing. God is not an individual of any sort. These passages stress an ethical dimension to language about God – questions of justice and mercy, right and wrong, wealth and poverty. They explore what it means for men and women to approach God if there is no individual being that we can identify, locate and direct ourselves towards. We will see in this chapter that the question of how we use the word 'God' must be understood as a dimension of our relationships with one another as men and women What did people mean when they used the word 'God' or rather in Hebrew 'El, 'Elohim, Adonai, Yahweh, and the other words that are used for the Creator? How are these words to be used rightly? And how can they be used wrongly? And what does this tell us about Israel's understanding of the word 'God'?

THE NAME OF NO ONE

Let us begin with the story in which God first reveals himself to Moses. In the book of Exodus we find Israel in captivity in Egypt, enslaved and oppressed by those in power. Not only were the Hebrews enslaved, but the Egyptian ruler had given orders to kill all new-born Hebrew males at birth: 'Every son that is born to the Hebrews you shall cast into the Nile, but you shall let every daughter live' (Exodus1:22). Moses had survived this genocidal policy as an infant by being set adrift in the river in a basket, and then found and raised by Pharaoh's daughter. Some years later, Moses 'saw an Egyptian beating a Hebrew, one of his people. He ... killed the Egyptian and hid him in the sand' (2:12). Then, fearing the anger of Pharoah, Moses fled eastward into the land of Midian where he stayed. It is there in the desert that Moses had his terrifying and illuminating encounter with God.

> And the angel of the Lord appeared to him in a flame of fire out of the midst of a bush; and he looked, and lo, the bush was burning, yet it was not consumed. And Moses said, 'I will turn aside and see this great sight, why the bush is not burnt.' When the Lord saw that he turned aside to see, God called to him out of the bush: 'Moses, Moses!' And he said, 'Here am I.' Then he said, 'Do not come near; put off your shoes from your feet, for the place on which you are standing is holy ground.' And he said, 'I am the God of your father, the God of Abraham, the God of Isaac, and the God of Jacob.' And Moses hid his face, for he was afraid to look at God (3:2-6).

God now reveals himself as the liberator of the children of Israel: 'I have heard their cry,' he says, and 'I have seen the oppression'. And so he calls Moses to deliver Israel from bondage, promising to be with him as he does so. And it is now, when Moses asks who this God is – the God of his ancestors – and by what name he should speak of him to the people of Israel, God replies:

'*I am who I am*.' And God said to Moses, 'Say to the people of Israel, "*I am* has sent me to you"' (3:14).[9]

The story seems at first sight to be about the 'name' of God, but if it were a story about the naming of God then we might be tempted to see the God so named as an individual being called *'ehyeh*. After all, we name other individuals – our family, friends, neighbours. We distinguish people from each other in speech and writing by naming them, so that we and others know who we are referring to. I call one of my sons Dominic and the other one Isaac, so that my hearers can tell one from the other when I am talking about them. If this story in Exodus were about naming an individual being, it would help people distinguish the God of Israel from 'other gods. But this story does not actually give God a name in the ordinary sense. It is actually a grammatical utterance, a sentence: 'I am who I am'. This is not a name, and is hardly a distinguishing feature the way a name is. Any of us could say this of ourselves in fact: I am who I am. You are who you are. It does not enable us to identify one individual over against another, which is essential to a name. How would 'I am' distinguish the God of Israel from any of the other gods that Israel might once have thought existed? How would it distinguish the God of Israel, who is about to free Israel from slavery, from the gods of the Egyptians who have been helping the Egyptians – as they believe – to enslave the Israelites? The sentence is not like a name at all.

And this is hardly surprising. In the ancient Near East, as in many other cultures, naming something gave the person

---

[9] *ehyeh 'asher 'ehyeh'.* Because of the nature of 'tenses' in Hebrew grammar, this could equally well be translated, 'I will be who (or what) I shall be'. It is possible that the second occurrence of the Hebrew verb *'ehyeh* was originally intended as a causative form of the verb to be. So the phrase might mean 'I am who causes to exist' or something of that sort. Though this might be an interesting line to pursue, I will not pursue it here but will discuss the sentence in the sense that translators and commentators have made of it for centuries.

naming it a degree of control over the thing named. So in the second chapter of Genesis (2:20) where we read that God allowed Adam to name all the animals, we should understand that humanity was thus being given dominion over them, as stated more explicitly in Genesis 1:28. This also applied to naming people: in many of the contemporary cultures, knowing the name of a person allowed you to harm him or her – which is why members of some communities had secret or taboo names which were not told to others who might use their name to harm them. Naming their gods was also thought to give people access to them and influence over them. So in Egyptian legend Isis was thought to have manipulated the god Ra, asking, 'Can I not, by using the sacred name of Ra, make myself mistress of the earth?' When Egyptians prayed to Isis, they urged her to 'use the true name of Ra' in order to get what they wanted. Perhaps this is why Moses anticipates that when he tells the Israelites that God has sent him, they will ask, 'What is his name?' They want access to – and influence over – divine power. But this is also why God refuses to give a name in the ordinary sense. 'I am who I am' is not a name like this. If it were a name, it would enable us to list the God of Israel alongside the gods of the nations – Isis, Ra, Astarte, Marduk and so on. Then the Creator would be an individual, a god competing with other gods for honour or sacrifice. But the God of Israel cannot compete. Isis and Ra competed with each other, just as we saw the gods struggled and interacted in Akkadian legend, because they were imagined as distinct things or beings. But the Creator is not one of the things that exist. The God of Israel is not any thing.

Of course in the Exodus story God *seems* to be saying that this is a personal name. He says, 'This is my name for all time; by this name I shall be invoked for all generations to come', but it really does not function like a name. It is a verb, and it goes through the changes that verbs go through. The word that God originally uses for himself is, *ehyeh*, 'I am', but when the Jews talk about him, they use a different form of the verb, 'He is' (*Yahweh*). God says, 'I am', while Israel says, 'He is'. These are first-person and third-person verbs in the imperfect tense. Names don't normally have this kind of grammar. The grammar of this *Ehyeh,* or *Yahweh* means that it behaves more like a statement than a name – albeit a rather puzzling and strange statement.

God's self-revelation as 'I am' or 'He is' was later taken up by early Christian and medieval authors, and by some modern writers, struggling to make sense of it. They recognised the strangeness of the utterance. What did God mean by this, 'I am who I am'? For many writers this 'I am' was understood to mean something extraordinary about God's 'existence', something which made it quite unlike the existence of existing things. For Thomas Aquinas, for example, this 'I am who I am' suggested something that was uniquely true of God – that his defining essence was simply being or *esse.* For every individual thing, to be at all was to be a particular kind of thing. Each thing had its own nature, its own defining qualities. It also had existence – not as a 'property' but simply in the sense that some thing with a particular set of properties either existed or it did not. Horses, with their nature (big hairy hoofed quadrupeds) do actually exist. Existence isn't part of their nature. Their nature is to do with what *kind* of thing they are. Their existence is the fact *that* they are. Unicorns have a different nature (big hairy hoofed quadrupeds with a single horn), but they don't actually exist. That doesn't affect their nature; it's just that nothing with that nature actually exists. In other words, the nature of a thing and its being are two quite different ways of talking. Some things have natures and don't exist – i.e. they are not things at all. Other things have natures and also exist, and so are real things, a coming together of nature and existence. But God is not like this for Aquinas. For him God is 'sheer being' or 'being itself' (*esse tantum*[10]), not an existing thing which

[10]   *De ente et essentia*, Cap. IV, §27.

would be a compound of nature and existence. For Aquinas God is simply being itself, his existence *is* his nature: not 'a being' (*ens*, a noun) but 'to be' (*esse*, the infinitive form of the verb).[11] Other writers have reflected on this Exodus story too, and have read it as pointing towards God as 'the ground of being', for example, rather than any particular existing being.[12] But there's something else about this story, and the great 'I am'. The mystery of God is defined by something that is not God. The sentence 'I am who I am' is shortly followed by the announcement of freedom from slavery. By a promise:

> 'I promise that I will bring you up out of the affliction of Egypt, to the land of the Canaanites, the Hittites, the Amorites, the Perizzites, the Hivites and the Jebusites, a land flowing with milk and honey.' (3:17)

So this revelation of the-name-which-is-not-a-name invites us to see that the word 'God' is not a way of distinguishing one being from other individuals who might be confused with him. The meaning of 'God' is not determined by a name, whether 'I am', or 'He is'. The meaning is found in a concrete historical and political situation, in the process of liberation that emerges from encountering God. Slaves are freed, oppressors are cast down, and Israel is led to its promised land. The moment of revelation is therefore about what God *creates* in human history. Much as we saw in the last chapter, that the Creation story is not really a story about God, but a story about all the things that exist, and how they are created by the Creator; so this story about Moses and the burning bush answers the question, 'Who is Israel's God?' But it answers it not with a description or with a name which identifies some individual,

[11] *Summa Theologiae* 1a. 11. 4. *ipsum esse subsistens.* See Burrell 1979, 7, 42-54.
[12] Paul Tillich is the modern theologian chiefly associated with the phrase 'ground of being'.

but with an account of God as liberator – i.e. in what he brings about, rather than what he is in himself.

This same way of identifying God is taken up again and again, most dramatically in Exodus 20:1. This is a critical moment of revelation, the moment when God forms a covenant with Israel and issues the Law. The passage starts off with that name again – which is not a name. God speaks: 'I [am] *He* [who] *is*, your God (*'anochi yahweh 'eloheika*) , who brought you out of the land of Egypt, out of the house of slaves ...'. When God says 'I', referring to himself, he is identified by what he has done – the liberation of Israel. If he were an individual being, one individual as opposed to another individual, he would be characterised like any other individual by having this name rather than another name, having this identity rather than another identity, being like this rather than like that. But he is not an individual. His presence is characterised not by an individuating property of his own, but by the process of liberation which he has created and which Israel is now reflecting on. Israel wants to see, but there is nothing there to see – except for the things that God has done for Israel: 'who brought you out of the house of slaves'. Israel is asking, 'what does it mean that we have been freed from slavery?' and is coming up with theological answers. She is coming up with a mystery, something incomprehensible, and is calling this mystery 'God'. It's very like the question Israel asked by Genesis, 'What does it mean that the world exists, rather than nothing existing?' and she called this mystery 'God'.

IMAGES OF GOD

Having introduced himself as the liberator, God gives the first of the ten commandments on Mount Sinai: 'You shall have no other gods'. And then the second commandment states:

'You shall not make for yourself a graven image, or any likeness of anything that is in heaven above, or that is in

43

the earth beneath, or that is in the water under the earth; you shall not bow down to them or serve them; for I the Lord your God am a jealous God ....' (20:4).

The prohibition of images is important from our point of view, for this is not just the prohibition of images of *other* gods. Of course, they were prohibited too; you mustn't make a graven image of Enkidu or Astarte, Isis or Ra, Moloch or Ba'al, or any of the gods that were around. But neither must you make an image of Yahweh, the God of Israel. Why is this? Is it because the Israelites were, like other ancient peoples in the near east, confused between the image and the reality? Is it because if they used graven images, statues and pictures, they would worship the object itself rather than the divine reality it represented? Some writers have suggested that the prohibition of graven images is precisely for this reason: because these ancient people were so primitive that they couldn't tell the difference between an image and the god it represented. But research into Ancient Near Eastern culture has shown precisely the opposite: people of that period did not identify the visible image with the deity they worshipped.[13] They were not tempted to worship the image *as image*. They used the image to express something about the divinity it represented.

So why are images – including images of Yahweh – prohibited? One way to explore the prohibition is through the lens of Deuteronomy 4:12-15:

Then the Lord spoke to you out of the midst of the fire; *you heard the sound of words, but saw no form. There was only a voice.*

And he declared to you his covenant, which he commanded you to perform, that is, the ten commandments; and he wrote them upon two tablets of

---

[13]   Von Rad, 1966, 144-65.

stone. And the Lord commanded me at that time to teach you statutes and ordinances, that you might do them in the land which you are going over to possess.

Therefore take good heed to yourselves. Since you saw no form on the day that the Lord spoke to you at Horeb (Sinai) out of the midst of the fire, beware lest you act corruptly by making a graven image for yourselves, in the form of any figure, the likeness of male or female, the likeness of any beast that is on the earth.

In Deuteronomy the prohibition of images is rooted in the giving of the law itself. You can't have images of God because God hasn't revealed himself as an object of sight, or any object which could be represented by an image. He has revealed himself simply by giving the Law. In other words, the meaning of the word 'God' is not to be found in wondering what kind of thing he is (as he isn't any kind of thing) and how that thing might be represented, but in asking what he commands. The answer to the question 'Who is God?' is not to be found by identifying a particular individual (as distinct from another individual), either by name or by image. It is to be found in God's commandments, such as 'You shall not kill', 'You shall not steal', 'Love the sojourner, for you were sojourners in the land of Egypt'. You identify God not by looking up at heaven, or at an image, but by looking round at your fellow men and women and by asking how we should live together – above all in the commandments of justice and mercy which we have *heard*. It is by hearing and obeying his commandments that Israel is to approach the question of God.

We'll come back to this issue of justice and the meaning of the word 'God' later on. But for the moment let's look at what happens in the Bible when people do make images. There is an interesting passage in the book of Judges (17: 1-6) where a Hebrew makes an image of God:

There was a man of the hill country of Ephraim, whose name was Micah.[14]

And he said to his mother, 'The eleven hundred pieces of silver which were stolen from you, about which you uttered a curse, and also spoke it in my ears, behold the silver is with me. I took it.'

And his mother said, 'May my son be blessed by Yahweh.'

And he returned the eleven hundred pieces of silver to his mother;

and his mother said, 'I consecrate the silver to Yahweh from my hand for my son, to make a graven image and a molten image; now I restore it to you.'

So when he returned the money to his mother, his mother took two hundred pieces of silver, and gave it to the silversmith, who made it into a graven image and a molten image; and it was in the house of Micah. And the man Micah had a shrine, and he made an ephod and a teraphim, and installed one of his sons, who became his priest.

In those days there was no king in Israel, and every man did what was right in his own eyes.

---

[14] His full name in Hebrew can be rendered as *Michaihu*, which means 'who is like Yahweh?' The answer to this question clearly *ought* to be 'no-one'. But this man makes an image, something which is meant to be 'like Yahweh', so that his name is denied by his deed; reality contradicts language. The book of Judges is in part about this kind of disintegration, and it's clearly manifest here. The disjunction between language and reality also appears in chapter 8 and 9, for the men of Israel say to Gideon, 'Rule over us, you and your son and your grandson', but he refuses. 'I will not rule over you, and my son will not rule over you....' (8:22-3). But he has a son and calls him Abimelech, which means 'my father is king' (8:31). He then declares himself king and kills all but one of his seventy brothers, slaying them on a single stone (9:1-6) in a grim parody of royal sacrifice. The sole survivor curses Abimelech and his supporters at Shechem, and Shechem is destroyed, and Abimelech is killed by a woman dropping a stone – a single stone - on his head (9:53). 'Thus God requited the crime of Abimelech' (9:56).

Now note that Micah is an Israelite, and that he and his mother worship Yahweh, the one God, the God of Israel. When her son stole the money, she cursed the thief. Now that he has confessed to her, she forgives him – but as she has cursed her son, calling down God's anger on him, she now wants to undo the curse. So she says first of all, 'May my son be blessed by the Lord' ('by Yahweh'). And then she dedicates 200 of these silver pieces to Yahweh again, to make an image. There is no reason to suppose that the image was anything other than an image of Yahweh. And at this point in the story there is very little explicit hint of disapproval. Only that last verse, 'every man did what was right in his own eyes' – points to a kind of general moral chaos. In other words, these were faithful Israelites, who made an image of Yahweh because they just didn't know any better.

But this story has to be read in a wider context as well. Only a few lines earlier we read about the capture and death of Samson. Samson is the great defender of Israel against the Philistines. He is God's chosen one, a hero, but he is betrayed into the hands of his enemies by the treachery of Delilah. And she is persuaded to betray him by the lords of the Philistines who tell her that if she helps them to overpower Samson, they will each give her money – eleven hundred pieces of silver; exactly the sum that Micah would steal from his mother (16:5). Is this a coincidence? The rabbis read this text as suggesting that Micah's mother was Delilah. The eleven hundred silver pieces he stole from her are the silver she got for betraying Samson. And then later in the book of Judges, after the story we've just read, some men from the tribe of Dan come and steal Micah's image of Yahweh, and take it with them, along with the priest who serves it. They take the image to Laish, 'to a people who were quiet and unsuspecting, and they smote them with the edge of the sword and burned the city with fire. .... and then they rebuilt the city and lived in it.'

So the story about Micah making an image of Yahweh is

stitched into a wider context by a particular quantity of silver. The silver starts off as a bribe to Delilah, who hands an innocent man over to his persecutors. Then it is stolen from the woman (supposedly Delilah) by her own son – which is another crime. Then she has it made into an idol – another crime. Then it is stolen by the bloodthirsty tribesmen of Dan, and used in the destruction of an innocent city and the murder of its people. One injustice after another.

And this little group of stories centring on the silver is stitched into an even larger context – almost the whole of the book of Judges – in which Israel is shown in a kind of moral disintegration and social disintegration. It is a disintegration mapped by human bodies. The book begins with Adonibezek, a Canaanite king whose household included 'seventy kings with their thumbs and big toes cut off' – thus mutilated they could no longer be warriors, and the cities they had ruled were symbolically and practically subjugated. Adonibezek is in turn defeated and captured by Israelites (1:6), and he himself has his thumbs and big toes cut off as he is reduced to slavery. So it begins with bodily disintegration, and this is appallingly amplified by the injustice and violence of a lawless land, so that in the end the last terrible violence takes place when a concubine is killed by Benjaminites from Gibeah, and her body is then cut into twelve pieces and the pieces are sent 'throughout all the territory of Israel' (19:29). As a result the tribe of Benjamin is 'cut off' from Israel and destroyed. This mounting cycle of violence, cruelty and injustice, the tribes of Israel massacring each other, leads therefore to the dismemberment of Israel itself. And all along there is that repeated refrain, 'each man did what was right in his own eyes'.

This tale of violence and destruction is the context for the silver idol of Yahweh in the Book of Judges. What happens when you have an image is you think that it gives you some connection to God; you think you can gain access to him by sacrificing in front of his image, by cult, priesthood, worship, prayer and so on. In this view an individual divine being is represented by the image in some way. It doesn't really matter from this point of view whether the god is represented by a silver statue or by a name. You are thinking of your god as an objective individual who is distinguished from other individual beings by its representation, and you think you can address yourself to this god *while at the same time doing deeds of injustice, betrayal, theft, violence.*

The story of Micah's image, then, is a challenge to the idea that there is any way of accessing the God of Israel except by doing justice. Or to put it another way, it is a challenge to the idea that the word 'God' means anything at all, unless you do justice. The meaning of the word is not like the meaning of a personal name. Personal names point our attention to individual beings. They distinguish one person from another. But the word 'God' doesn't point towards any individual. There is no such individual. The word 'God' is given meaning by what you *do* – not what you do to God, but what you do to other people in terms of justice and compassion as God has commanded.

FINDING THE TRUE IMAGE OF GOD

Just as human beings were forbidden to *make* images of God, they were also taught to recognise that there already *is* an image of God in the world made by God himself:

> God said, 'Let us make man in our image, after our likeness.' ... So God created man in his own image, in the image of God he created him, male and female he created them (Genesis 1:26-7).

The fact that every man and woman is made in the image of God, suggests another reason for the prohibition of graven images. Among the neighbouring societies you honoured the deity by honouring the image. But in Israel the only image of God is the human being. So in a sense you do honour the deity by honouring the image, but the image you honour is one made by God himself, not one made by human hands. And in particular the honour done to this image is linked to the rejection of violence:

> Whoever sheds the blood of man, by man shall his blood be shed; for God made man in his own image (Genesis 9:5).

Violence against human beings is the ultimate form of injustice and oppression, but it is also violence against God's own image. Only living human beings are permitted as images of God, and that image is honoured not by cult, but by the demand of respect and reverence that a person's very existence places on his or her neighbour. No man-made image can demand justice in this way, and every single human being stands to me not as an object but as a fellow-subject, as another person in relationship with me. Any image that cannot demand justice is an idol, an object. As Miranda says, if you worship God or anything at all without doing justice, 'at that moment God is no longer God. Man has made him into an idol.'[15]

TOWN PLANNING AND THE GOD OF ISRAEL

This connection between the word 'God' and the practice of justice becomes even more clearly stated in the prophetic writings in the Hebrew Bible. The prophet Amos gives us an important insight here. Amos lived and worked in the eighth century BC, in the middle of a booming economy in northern Israel where wealth and security seemed to be taken for granted – by some at least. It is interesting to look at the archaeological evidence for this period too. A French scholar called Roland de

---

[15]   Miranda, 1977, 40.

Vaux excavated the ancient biblical site of Tirzah (now called *Tell el-Far'ah*) which was an important city of the northern Kingdom of Israel during the lifetime of Amos, in the area where Amos was prophesying. In his excavations De Vaux discovered changes in the way the town was built and organised during that period. From around 900 BC, in the century before Amos, de Vaux says. 'houses appear which stand in an orderly fashion along well-marked streets. ... All the houses follow more or less the same arrangement and have roughly the same dimensions. Each represents the home of an Israelite family, and the very uniformity of the dwellings shows that there was no great social inequality among the inhabitants.' In addition to this social equality, De Vaux's excavation revealed all the houses of the town were gathered together by a defensive wall which encircled the town, creating a single community.

But the next stratum of archaeology is quite different. In the eighth century material, from around the time of Amos, we see signs of economic division. Now there are very large stone houses appearing, 'palaces' or 'patrician houses' for the rich in the northern part of the town, while to the south are the inferior houses of the poor which lacked proper foundations and had thin unstable walls. Furthermore, the surrounding wall which had formerly united the city, declaring it to be a single community with shared defences, had by now fallen into decay. Instead the town was divided, rich versus poor. The archaeology of the town reveals a society divided along fault lines of wealth and social status, losing its sense of shared identity.

This archaeology of division in Israel during the life-time of Amos corresponds to the picture painted by his own prophecies. This is how he describes his own society, the society of Israel:

> *Because they sell the righteous for silver,*
> *and the needy for a pair of shoes;*
> *they trample the head of the poor into the dust of the earth,*

and turn aside the way of the afflicted;
a man and his father go in to the same maiden,
so that my holy name is profaned;
they lay themselves down beside every altar
upon garments taken in pledge ....[16]
Hear this word, you cows of Bashan,
who are in the mountain of Samaria,
who oppress the poor, who crush the needy ...
They hate him who reproves at the gate,
and they abhor him who speaks the truth.
Therefore because you trample upon the poor
and take from him exactions of wheat,
you have built houses of hewn stone,
but you shall not dwell in them....
For I know how many are your transgressions,
and how great are your sins,
you who afflict the righteous, who take a bribe,
and turn aside the needy in the gate (2:6-8; 4:1, 5:10-12).

This is why Amos, speaking in God's name, utters the warning of punishment:

Smite the capitals until the thresholds shake,
and shatter them on the heads of the people;
and what are left of them I will slay with the sword;
not one of them shall flee,
not one of them shall escape (9:1).

Amos foretells the destruction of Israel, the slaughter of its people and its captivity and exile (and it is interesting that he

---

[16]   This is explicitly forbidden in Exodus 22:26 as a cruel form of exploitation of the poor: 'If ever you take your neighbour's garment in pledge, you shall restore it to him before the sun goes down; for that is his only covering, it is his mantle for his body; in what else shall he sleep? And if he cries to me, I will hear, for I am compassionate.'

does so partly in terms relating to architecture and planning: the town gates, houses of hewn stone, capitals and thresholds). And all this is the consequence of a moral failure of the wealthy:

> Woe to those who lie upon beds of ivory
> and stretch themselves upon their couches,
> and eat lambs from the flock
> and calves from the midst of the stall;
> who sing idle songs to the sound of the harp,
> and like David invent for themselves musical instruments;
> who drink wine in bowls
> and anoint themselves with the finest oils,
> but are not grieved over the ruin of Joseph. (6:4-6)

There is no suggestion here that there is anything intrinsically wrong with comfortable furniture, eating lambs or singing songs. Rather, as the final line of that passage shows, the denunciation comes because these pleasures are pursued by the wealthy without regard for the poor. In fact they are made possible for the wealthy precisely because they have so successfully exploited and oppressed their own people, taking bribes, trading with false measures, seizing the homes and lands of poor farmers. It is because his society has abandoned justice, dividing itself into rich and poor, a division created and sustained by the violence of the powerful against the humble, that Amos prophesies that Israel is going to be destroyed, led away into exile and slavery.

But for our present purposes of exploring Israel's theology and what people mean when they say the word 'God', Amos says something even more interesting – speaking 'in God's voice':

> I hate, I despise your feasts,
> and I take no delight in your solemn assemblies.
> Though you offer me your burnt offerings and cereal
>   offerings,

I will not accept them.
I will not look upon
the peace offerings of your fatted beasts.
Take away from me the noise of your songs;
to the melody of your harps I will not listen.
But let justice roll down like waters,
and righteousness like an everflowing stream. (5:21-4)

For this decadent Israel, the presence of God was expressed through prayer, by offerings made on his altar, by singing hymns and psalms in his praise. But Amos prophesies not only that Israel is going to be destroyed, but that she has already lost contact with God. Her prayers, psalms, music, sacrifices, offerings – none of these are acting as they should, as practices of the presence of God.

We saw that graven images are prohibited because they represent God as an individual who can be approached, identified as a particular individual being, conceptualised and objectified. In the same way having a cult can also fall into this trap – even a cult *without* graven images. All the drama of worship, prayer, sacrifice, and liturgy is a kind of address to God made *as if to an individual being*, someone who can be approached and identified, someone you can sing to or make offerings to. These activities are dramatic enactments of faith. But what happens to cult if it is uprooted from the practice of justice? There is no suggestion that graven images were being used among Amos's community, but they have nevertheless made God into an idol by making him into a mere object, an object of cult, a being who is simply 'there' and available when they perform the songs and the rituals, while they fail to hear and respond to his *voice*, which commands justice. As the Mexican theologian José Porfirio Miranda observes:

While there is injustice among a people, worship and prayer do not have Yahweh as their object, even though we have the formal and sincere "intention" of addressing ourselves to the true God. To know Yahweh is to do justice and compassion and right to the needy. If it were a question of a god, there would be no dilemma. The essence of the idol is that we can approach it directly. It is entity.... It is not the implacable moral imperative of justice. The question is not whether someone is seeking God or not, but whether s/he is seeking him where God himself has said that he is. If we prescind from the cry of the poor who seek justice, by objectifying God and believing that, because he is [a] being, he is there as always, since being is objective and does not depend on any considerations of our minds nor on what we can or cannot do, at that very moment he is no longer God but an idol.[17]

Miranda's remarks help us to understand Amos's criticism of cult as pointing towards our idea of God as Nothing. The temptation to make God into a being, something you can access by naming him, or by cult, or by representation, is to reduce him to an idol. The only God the prophet Amos is interested in is one who cannot be identified as an individual. God is the Unknown who utters an insistent demand for justice, who has chosen the poor and oppressed, who simultaneously promises their liberation and demands a liberating way of life among his people.

KNOWING GOD

This also connects us to the way the Hebrew prophets speak about 'knowing God'. To know an individual person I must know his or her name, or where he lives, or the way she thinks, or what political or social views she has, or the kind of music

17   Miranda 1977, 57-8.

he listens to, and what he does with his children at weekends, what she likes to eat. Perhaps I know things about this person's past, where he was born, who her father was. If I don't know any of these things, or things like these, I can hardly be said to know him or her. When you know an individual person or a thing, you have *information*; you know things about that individual. But though the prophets *often* talk about 'knowing God', they make it clear that they are not talking about this kind of knowing. Knowing God is not encountering him as an individual. Knowing God does not imply having information about God – what he is like. There isn't any information about what God is like; and God does not have a life-story.

Usually, knowing an individual being is a relationship between two individuals, the knower and the person known. But when the prophets speak about someone 'knowing God' it is not a relationship between that person and God as the individual object of their knowledge – because there is no such individual. When they talk about 'knowing God' they refer us not to God, but to other men and women. So Jeremiah says:

> Woe to him who builds his house by unrighteousness, and his upper rooms by injustice ... Did your father not eat and drink and do justice and righteousness? This is good. He judged the cause of the poor and the needy. This is good. *Is not this what it is to know me?* It is the Lord who speaks (22:15-16).

Knowing God is not knowing an individual being called 'God', but hearing and keeping his commandments by doing justice to human beings, men and women who are the living images of God. Similarly in the prophecy of Hosea, God says:

> *What I want is mercy, not sacrifice;*
> *knowledge of the Lord, not holocausts.* (6:6)

Here again knowledge of the Lord has nothing to do with information about God or having a personal encounter through religious ritual. It is equated with mercy – which is a kind of justice.[18]

Likewise *not* knowing God clearly does not mean that you have a lack of information about the heavenly being. When Hosea says that people have no knowledge of God, he's not complaining that they are ignorant about this individual being, that they haven't got enough information about God. Their ignorance of God is determined by one thing, and one thing only: their injustice.

> *There is no faithfulness or kindness,*
> *and no knowledge of God in the land.*
> *There is false swearing, lying, killing, stealing, adultery;*
> *they break all bounds and murder follows murder.*
> *(Hosea 4:1-2)*

Like 'knowing God', what the prophets mean by 'not knowing God' is not something that goes on between people and God, but rather something that goes on among people themselves. Justice and injustice lie in the domain of the human, the social, the historical. God is not part of that domain, nor of any other domain.

Even if we have the right songs, offer the right sacrifices, know the right religious formulae, if we act unjustly then Amos tells us we are not worshipping the living God of Israel, the Creator. Even if we call the object of our devotion 'God' or Yahweh, it is nevertheless an idol or false god. And the implication of this is something that we shall be noting

---

[18]   This couplet uses a very common form in Hebrew poetry, where one line effectively repeats the first line with some variation. In these two lines God wants, 'A not B, C not D'. B and D are more or less the same thing ('sacrifice' and 'holocausts'), and so A and C are likewise proposed as the same thing: 'mercy' and 'knowledge of the Lord'.

again in this book: *the real opposition to faith is not atheism, but idolatry.* There are occasional references to atheism in the Bible, but even there the problem with the 'atheist' is not that he or she is a rational philosophical speculator who has come to the 'wrong' conclusion. Consider Psalm 10, for example:

> *The wicked boasts of the desires of his heart,*
> *and the man greedy for gain curses and renounces the Lord.*
> *In the pride of his countenance the wicked does not seek*
>   *him;*
> *all his thoughts are, 'There is no God.'*

The question of the wicked man's atheism is rather marginal, at best. It is his greed for gain that troubles the Psalmist, the fact that 'the wicked hotly pursue the poor', or 'his mouth is filled with cursing, deceit and oppression ... he sits in ambush in the villages; in hiding places he murders the innocent .... he lurks that he may seize the poor'. Of course, one may argue that the wicked man does all these things *because* he is an atheist and so is not restrained by fear of God, but that is a rather abstract explanation; the real point of the Psalmist's complaint is the man's violence. His 'atheism' is not regarded as bad because it is a mistaken philosophy in some abstract metaphysical discourse. His 'atheism' is demonstrated by his violence. (In which case might we not argue that people who do justice and act mercifully demonstrate their faithfulness to God – even if they profess to be atheists?) In the end, the question of the existence or non-existence of a being called 'God' is not what the Psalmist is concerned about. Again, the question of 'God' collapses into the question of mercy and justice among people.

CHAPTER THREE.

JESUS, LANGUAGE AND PRACTICE

IN THE PRECEDING chapters we have looked at aspects of the Hebrew Bible. We have considered the doctrine of Creation, and the idea that if God is the Creator of everything that exists then God cannot be 'one of the things which exist'. His 'being' is not that of a merely existing thing. We have also explored Israel's idea of justice as a way of understanding the meaning and use of the word 'God'. If 'God' is not the name of any object or individual being, it follows that there is nothing 'there' to worship; but worship is realised in those who hear God's call to justice. This idea of 'God' frees us from idolatry, for if God were some individual being whose existence was simply 'there', then we could name it, direct our attention towards it and worship it. But God is not approachable in that way – the way an individual person, or a hat-stand, or a boulder are approachable objects of attention. So we must attend to God and approach him not by looking towards *him* (for there is no direction that counts as 'looking towards God') but by looking towards each other and the way we live our lives, and by opening our ears to his call to live in justice and mercy. If we don't do that, then our worship – even if we tell ourselves that we are praying to Yahweh, the God of Abraham, Isaac and Jacob – will actually be a form of idolatry. Even if you are a monotheist, even if you take the holy name of God on your lips, if you are not doing justice and acting mercifully you are simply not praying to the living God. In that case, whatever you worship is an idol.

But Jesus is a man. And a man certainly *is* an individual thing, a being in time and space. Even if we accept all that we have said about God, *as God*, how can it be said to apply for Christians, for whom Jesus Christ is the eternal and unchanging Word of God but is also a human being? 'The Word was made flesh, and dwelt among us.' This means that the unchanging and eternal Nothing, who cannot be an object or any kind of thing, has entered into the history of the world he created. Christians believe that in the person of Christ, who *was* a particular individual, God lived and walked in particular places, ate and drank, spoke and sang, suffered and died. God has become a something – and more than a something, a someone. A human being. We may be able to speak of God as 'Nothing'; but can we speak of Christ in this way, since as well as being divine and worthy of the worship that is only given to God, he is also clearly 'something'?

DE-OBJECTIFYING JESUS

In so far as Christ is an individual human being with his own individual biography, we clearly cannot call him 'Nothing' in the same way as we do when we speak more generally of God. But I would suggest that the New Testament also plays with the idea of God as Nothing, even in relation to the human person that is Christ – presumably because it is concerned with how the human Jesus is the image and presence of the living God. It is an idea that Jesus himself takes up at various moments, and so do some of his early followers. So we will look at a few of these passages first, and then will move onto another aspect of the New Testament.

First, we may consider the question of justice and mercy, or if you like the question of love, which is the more common way of expressing it in the Gospels, but comes to much the same thing. Is it possible that just as 'God' can be treated as an idol in the Old Testament, when he is worshipped by those who care nothing for the poor, so Jesus himself can be treated as an idol in the New Testament? It is a slightly different issue here, of course, given that Christ *as man* is an individual being, while God *as God* is not. But the Gospels still suggest that Jesus can be treated as an idol. This is an idea that seems to be raised in Matthew's Gospel, where Jesus says:

> Not everyone who says to me, 'Lord, Lord,' shall enter the kingdom of heaven, but the person who does the will of my Father who is in heaven. On that day many will say to me, 'Lord, Lord, did we not prophesy in your name, and cast out demons in your name, do many mighty works in your name?' Then I shall declare to them, 'I have never known you; away from me, you evil men!' (Matthew 7:21-3)

First of all, note that this passage is the culmination of a long teaching in Matthew about what disciples should be like: they should be poor, gentle, merciful, peacemakers. They must not only obey the Law, but radically internalise the justice that lies at the heart of the Law. They must not exercise any kind of violence. They mustn't even defend themselves. They must give alms, and must do so in secret. They must not build up riches. They must not judge or condemn people. In short, they are given a manifesto for the works of justice and mercy. And this is what Jesus means in the passage here about doing 'the will of my Father'. It is not those who call Jesus 'Lord, Lord', who cry out to this individual being, who enter the kingdom, but those who *live* like this, justly and mercifully. Jesus is quite specifically *excluding* from the kingdom those who treat him as an idol – *away from me, you evil men!* These are people who think that calling on him, or even doing fantastic things in his name – prophesying, performing miracles and so on – is what access to God in Christ is about. But *he* says that what he is about is justice and mercy. To worship Christ without justice and mercy is again a kind of idolatry, even though Christ is an individual and is a potential object of our attention.

This is suggested at other points in the Gospels, where the question of justice and mercy is the defining issue, and the critical question about who Christ is – who he is for us. Consider the passage in Matthew's gospel about the last judgement. Jesus is talking about his own second coming, how he will judge the whole world:

> When the Son of Man comes in his glory, and all the angels with him, then he will sit on his glorious throne. All the nations will be gathered before him and he will separate them one from another, as a shepherd separates the sheep from the goats. He will place the sheep on his right hand and the goats on his left.
>
> Then the King will say to those on his right hand, 'Come, you whom my Father has blessed, inherit the kingdom prepared for you from the foundation of the world. For I was hungry and you gave me food; I was thirsty and you gave me drink; I was a stranger and you welcomed me; I was naked and you clothed me; I was sick and you visited me; I was in prison and you came to me.'
>
> Then the righteous will answer him, 'Lord, when did we see you hungry and feed you; or thirsty and give you drink? When did we see you a stranger and welcome you, or naked and clothe you? And when did we see you sick or in prison and visit you?'
>
> And the King will answer them, 'Truly, I say to you, as you did it to one of the least of these brothers or sisters of mine, you did it to me.' (Matthew 25:31-40)

And of course he goes on to say the same thing, but in reverse, to the 'goats', to the damned who have not fed the hungry or welcomed the homeless poor. Here the whole question of encounter with Christ is re-defined as encounter with the poor, the naked, the hungry, the outcast. This is the saving encounter with Christ: not meeting him as an individual person, a divine being who will reward you if you treat him well. You encounter Christ precisely when you encounter someone else – the hungry and thirsty and the sick and prisoners. You encounter the divine being whom you worship when you encounter and respond to the poor and the powerless. That doesn't mean that the hungry and the homeless are gods. It means that what counts as a response to God-in-Christ is the response you make to someone else – your poor neighbour – who is also an individual being. What counts as an encounter with God-in-Christ is the quality of tenderness in your encounter with those who need you. In this *moral* sense, just as God is not an individual among other individuals, our encounter with Christ is not simply an encounter with one individual among others; rather it is constituted by an encounter with those others. In this sense, Christ is not just one other person, alongside the hungry, the thirsty, the sick, the imprisoned.

And it is significant in this story that the 'sheep' and 'goats' are astonished when they are spoken to like this. Those who fed the hungry and so on did so not in order to welcome Christ, for they say, 'When did we see you hungry and feed you?' They had no idea that this was an encounter with Christ. They certainly were not treating the hungry individual in front of them as a means to an end, as a means of approaching a different individual – Christ – for they had no idea that their response to this hungry person had anything to do with Christ. That phrase, 'When did we see you hungry?' implies that their attention was focussed entirely on the hungry person in front of them, not on Christ. They were not dealing out sandwiches to the hungry while looking over their shoulder to see if Christ or God was watching, in order to earn a reward. They are welcomed into the house of the Father because getting a reward from the Father was not part of any calculus in their giving. They did not seek a reward other than the truth of their relationship with the hungry person.

And here we may look at another example of the same kind of thing, this time not from the words of Christ but from the words of St Paul. Paul is writing to the church in Corinth. The church in that town is clearly divided. There are rich householders who seem to be throwing their weight around and lording it over their fellow Christians; and there are 'Chloe's people' as Paul calls them, who are slaves. It is a division between rich and poor, powerful and powerless. Paul writes to them about the way they celebrate the Lord's Supper, where Christians come together and share bread and wine in memory of Christ's death and resurrection, believing that they are thereby sharing in the Lord's body and blood. Paul describes their celebration of the Lord's supper like this:

> When you assemble as a church, I hear that there are divisions among you. ... When you meet together, it is not the Lord's Supper that you eat. For in eating, each one goes ahead with his own meal, and one is hungry while another is drunk. What! Do you not have houses for eating and drinking in? Do you despise the church of God and humiliate those who have nothing? (1 Corinthians 11:17-22)

The point he is making is that the Lord's Supper is meant to be a sign of unity. You are meant to be one, because you belong to each other. Because, as he says in this letter, the church community itself is the body of Christ, and so it should be united. The division between rich and poor undermines that unity. If at this common meal the rich bring their own food and drink, and go ahead feasting together, while the poor are hungry and humiliated at the very meal which is meant to be a sign of their unity, then the unity of Christ's body is being broken, divided and violated. The body is the way that the rich belong to the poor, so when the rich fail to honour the poor, they are actually failing to recognise the body itself. So Paul goes on:

> Whoever eats and drinks without discerning the Body eats and drinks judgement upon himself. (1 Corinthians 11:29)

This again is a warning against idolatry. Just as you cannot worship Christ without showing justice and mercy to each other, so you can't have access to Christ in this most sacred meal which he established, unless you are prepared to let the meal teach you and transform you, to recognise how all members belong to each other, how they are called to be one body by sharing one bread and one cup, and so how they are called to love and support one another.

These passages seem to harmonize with what we saw in the Old Testament. There is a danger of idolatry, even in the worship of Christ, if we treat him *simply* as an object of worship, if we don't allow the love of Christ to draw us into that kingdom of justice and mercy towards one another. And if we do allow ourselves to be drawn in this way, then our union with Christ is not with him as an *object* to which we give our attention, but as the dynamic *subject* of our lives, so that Paul can say, 'It is no longer I who live, but Christ who lives in me' (Galatians 2:20).

JESUS TALKING: BEING AFRAID

There is another other aspect of the New Testament that sheds light on our sense of 'God as Nothing'. We find it in many of the utterances of Jesus as he speaks to his disciples, teaching them, weaving stories and pictures of the kingdom of God. It may seem at first sight that Jesus imagines God as an individual being or person. He uses the kind of language about God that people generally use about individuals (father, judge, vinedresser and so on), so that we might imagine that God was an individual who could be listed alongside other individual beings. He also seems to locate his Father in a particular place – 'heaven' – as though this were a place which could be listed alongside other places, and happens to be the place where God lives ('Our Father, who art in Heaven'). But if we look carefully at some of these utterances of Jesus and at the way he uses such images, we find once again that the word 'God' does not act as the name of one of the things that exist, the name of an individual being. He cannot be listed among or alongside existing things as if he were just another one. There is something peculiar about the way the grammar of Jesus's teaching works – what we might call his 'grammar of God' – which suggests that for Jesus too, God is Nothing. What follows in the rest of this chapter leans heavily on the work of the late Gareth Moore, in particular on his unpublished 1984 dissertation whose title I have shamelessly stolen for this book, 'God as Nothing' (Blackfriars, Oxford), and his subsequent *Believing in God: A Philosophical Essay* (Edinburgh, T&T Clark, 1988). Indeed, much of what follows is little more than a précis of some of the arguments in his 1984 work, and of ideas floated during discussions with him when he taught me in Oxford – exciting conversations which planted in my mind the seed of this book.

FEARING GOD

Let us look first at what Jesus says about 'fearing God'. This is pretty dramatic stuff, and at first sight the imagery seems to suggest that there is a particular individual called 'God' whom we should fear.

> 'Do not fear those who kill the body but cannot kill the soul. Rather fear him who can destroy both body and soul in hell. Are not two sparrows sold for a penny? Yet not one

of them will fall to the ground without your Father's will. But even the hairs of your head are all numbered. Fear not, therefore; you are of more value than many sparrows.' (Matthew 10:28-31)

Here we find an opposition between God and human beings. We are told to fear God, but not to fear human beings. At first sight that seems reasonable. God can hurt you more than human beings can. Human beings can torture you and kill you, but God can do all that and then cast you into hell and torture you for eternity. The contrast between God and man in this case is simply that God is like humans but more terrifying.

But if we read it like this, the logic of what Jesus is saying does not work. If two individuals threaten me, then I might well be afraid of both of them. I may be afraid of Angus, a neighbour of mine who is a bully and a nuisance. I know he doesn't like me, and I know he's pretty violent, so I fear him. In addition, he keeps telling me what to do, and threatening to give me a kicking if I don't do it.

But there is someone else in my neighbourhood who is much more violent than Angus. Harry is a gang leader in a violent criminal underworld, and with connections to hired killers. Various citizens in our part of town have disappeared in suspicious circumstances, and the police have not been able to find them. Harry is a vicious psychopath, and I know that if I cross him he will do far worse than beat me up. He is a threat not only to me, but also to my wife and children, while through his contacts he can make sure that I will never again be safe wherever I go. And to make matters worse, Harry also keeps telling me to do things, and the things that he tells me to do are precisely the opposite of what Angus tells me to do.

Naturally, I am inclined to obey Harry rather than Angus. I am vastly more afraid of Harry the psychopath than I am of Angus, who is just a bully. But being afraid of Harry does not stop me being afraid of Angus. It *is* possible to be afraid of two different people. I am afraid of both of them; it is simply that I am more afraid of Harry than I am of Angus. I fear Angus *in addition* to Harry, because they are two individuals - dreadful and terrifying individuals.

Now at first sight it *looks* as if Jesus is portraying God as simply an even more dangerous and violent and terrifying person than Harry or Angus. Here is some non-human person who can not only kill me, but can cast my body and soul into eternal torment. It seems that Jesus is depicting God as simply a kind of supreme and invisible gangster, a great celestial psychopath who is more terrifying, more violent, than either Harry or Angus; a being who can hurt me more than either of them can.

But it is clearly not the purpose of Jesus to reduce us all to trembling terrified subjects. Notice that telling phrase at the end of the passage: *'Fear not, therefore.'* That is hardly compatible with the image of God as an infinitely violent being. Certainly God is *pictured* in this passage as a terrifying and powerful tyrant, but you can tell that it is only a picture by the conclusions that Jesus draws from it: Fear not.

When talking about individuals, I *can* be afraid of two different people: Harry and Angus. I am more afraid of Harry than I am of Angus, but I am still afraid of Angus. I am afraid of one *in addition* to the other. They are two potential objects of fear. But 'fearing God' does not work in this way. Fearing Harry doesn't stop me fearing Angus, but fearing God **does** stop me fearing Harry or Angus or anybody else: 'fear not therefore'. I can be afraid of two different people, but I cannot be afraid of God and Harry at the same time. Because Harry and God are not two different people, not two individuals. If I fear God, then there is *nobody* I fear. I am not frightened of a visible individual man like Harry; nor am I frightened of some invisible individual called God. That is why following the saying about 'fearing God' Jesus talks immediately not about the terrible things God can do to you, but about God's care for human beings, how 'even the hairs of your head are numbered', how God values us. Fearing God means 'fearing *nobody*', means being unafraid.[19]

That is *not* to say that being unafraid is automatically the same as 'fearing God'. There are lots of circumstances where you might be unafraid, but you wouldn't be 'fearing God' in the way Jesus means. You might be on a desert island, where there is nobody to fear. You might be in a coma, and unable to fear anyone. You might be too drunk to recognise the threats you face. You might be so powerful and violent yourself that you feel no need to be afraid of anyone else. Or you might be so desperately unhappy that you think of death as a welcome release, and so you don't fear it. But in a certain *context*, in the context of a way of life which involved hope and trust and faith and love, you might say that not being afraid at all was a sign that you feared God in the sense that Jesus is talking about here. You cannot be a God-fearer and at the same time be afraid of anyone. As John tells us, reflecting on what it means to love God, 'There is no fear in love, for perfect love casts out fear' (1 John 4:18).

And let me add here that when we say 'fearing God' frees us from all fear, this is not because God will protect us from violence and cruelty. You might have argued that if you fear God you don't need to be afraid of other people like Harry and Angus, because God will protect you from them, so they cannot hurt you. But that is not what Jesus is saying. He is not saying that if you fear God then you get a kind of celestial protection package which will keep you safe from harm. On the contrary, he often stresses that if you follow him, if you believe and trust in God, you *will* be harmed: people will persecute you, betray you, put you to death (Luke 21:12; Matthew 10:16-18; John 16:2). The implication is not that you will be safe from human violence if you fear God. You will not

19   Moore 1984, 80-83.

be saved from any particular violent fate, but whatever violent fate does befall you, you will *still* be safe. Your protection is not that appalling things won't happen; your protection is that even when they do happen you are still safe, because you are in the arms of a loving Father. He watches the sparrows fall; he doesn't stop them falling. He loves his children, and he allows them to suffer and to die. So just as 'fearing God' means you are afraid of nothing and nobody, so 'God is protecting you' can be true when you have *nothing* to protect you. For the disciples, because they enjoy God's love and protection, everything is all right, even when *nothing* is all right.

JESUS TALKING: HEAVEN

Heaven is a funny kind of place, we might say. Or at least the language of heaven behaves in a strange sort of way. In some passages the Bible implies that heaven is something created: 'In the beginning God created the heavens and the earth' (Genesis 1:1). It is treated as simply part of the cosmos, part of the created order of things. As part of creation it clearly cannot contain God, you would have thought. But in other biblical passages we find a different picture, where 'heaven' or 'the heavens' is treated as if it were the name of the place where God lives – Psalm 11:4 tells us that 'the Lord's throne is in heaven', and from there 'his eyes see the children of men', while Jesus tells us, 'Your Father in heaven knows that you need all these things' (Matthew 6:32), and he taught us to pray, 'Our Father, who art in heaven'. The implication here – and in many other passages – seems to be that heaven and earth are two distinct places, and God occupies one of them and looks down at the other. This seems a bit strange. How can the Creator of everything and everywhere live in a particular place, one of the places which he has created? Of course, if God is the creator of everywhere he is in one sense present everywhere, his power filling and sustaining the universe (both heaven and earth); but on the other hand as the Creator of all places God cannot be contained in any of them, so in another sense he is nowhere. Therefore, as so often in the Bible, we have to treat the idea of God living in a particular place called 'heaven' as simply a picture. But if we explore the picture and look carefully at the way it is used, we will see that perhaps it is not meant as a literal description of 'reality' (whatever that might mean). We learn to read the image in different ways according to how the author is using it, according to the imagery and the purpose of the text.

In some circumstances it seems that the word 'heaven' is even used as a metaphor for God himself. So when we say, 'heaven knows where I'll get the money to pay this month's rent', we really mean 'God knows' (and of course, when we say, 'God knows' we are saying 'I don't know', and even 'no one knows'). When we say, 'Heaven knows', we are not ascribing knowledge to some place up in the sky or anywhere else. We are using the word 'heaven' to refer to God himself – a polite and reverend circumlocution.

Jesus has various things to say about 'heaven', and I am not going to argue that the word is only used in one way. But there are instances where he talks about 'heaven' in ways which shed light on the idea of God as Nothing.[20] Here is one such passage from Jesus' Sermon on the Mount:

> Do not lay up treasure for yourselves on earth, where moth and rust consume and where thieves break in and steal. But lay up for yourselves treasure in heaven, where neither moth nor rust consumes, and where thieves do not break in and steal. For where your treasure is, there will be your heart also. (Matthew 6:19-21)

Now it is actually perfectly possible for me to lay up treasure in two different places (just as it is possible for me to be afraid of

[20]   Moore 1984, 113-7.

two different people). I can lay up treasure in Glasgow, where I have an account in the Bank of Scotland, and at the same time I can lay up treasure in London, where my stockbroker invests some of my wealth in stocks and shares. I could also lay up quite a lot of treasure under my mattress at home. So it *is* possible to lay up treasure in several different places. And there are all kinds of activities that might count as 'laying up treasure' – keeping money in the bank, hiding precious objects under the bed, playing the stock-market, investing in antiques and fine art. They may all look quite different superficially: one consists in reading the financial news and pestering my stockbroker on the telephone, the other consists in going round car boot sales and junk shops, hoping to find a hitherto unidentified Rembrandt. But though these activities *look* different, they all count as 'laying up treasure' because they are all ways of acquiring treasure or wealth for myself.

So why is it not possible for me to lay up treasure both on earth *and* in heaven? If I can lay it up in two different places, why does Jesus say, 'do not lay it up on earth, but in heaven'? The clear implication of what he is saying is that you have to choose one or the other. This would not apply to laying up treasure in Glasgow and London, for in that case I do not have to choose one or the other; I can happily keep wealth in both places. That is because Glasgow and London can be added together to make two places. So can places closer together: my house and your house, under the mattress or behind the sofa. Distance is not relevant here. Any two places on earth are two places, and I can keep my treasure in one or other of them, or in both of them. But I cannot do this if one of those 'places' is heaven. There is no hint in this passage that you can lay up treasure in heaven and somewhere else at the same time. And that is because heaven is not a place alongside other places (just as God is not an individual alongside other individuals). It is not another place, because it is 'nowhere'. Thus, while I can ask how to get from Glasgow to London, I cannot ask (except in a joke) how to get from Glasgow to heaven. If you made a list of all the different places that exist, heaven would not be one of the places on that list, because the word 'heaven' doesn't refer to one place rather than another place.

Another difference between laying up treasure in heaven and laying it up in Glasgow is that if I want to lay up treasure in Glasgow there are certain things I have to do, what you might call treasure-laying-up activity – whether it's banking or stuffing wads of cash under the mattress. I have to do something that looks like laying up treasure. I have to amass some riches. But if I want to lay up treasure in heaven, there is no activity that I have to do which counts as 'laying-up-treasure'. I don't have to amass any riches at all. Instead I have to do the opposite, as Jesus says:

> Fear not, little flock, for it is your Father's good pleasure to give you the kingdom. Sell your possessions and give alms; provide yourselves with purses that do not grow old, with a treasure in the heavens that does not fail, where no thief approaches and no moth destroys. For where your treasure is, there will your heart be also. (Luke 12:32-4)

Clearly the way to lay up treasure in heaven is not to lay up treasure at all – anywhere! It is to sell your possessions and give away the proceeds in alms to the poor. We saw that fearing God is fearing nobody; now we see that having treasure in heaven is having treasure nowhere.

And notice that there is nothing automatic about this. Remember how we saw that fearing God was fearing nobody, but that fearing nobody was not automatically fearing God – you may be in a coma, on a desert island, and so on. It is a particular *kind* of not-fearing that counts as 'fearing God'; it must be a part of your whole way of life – trusting and generous. Similarly with laying up treasure, it isn't just *any* kind of not-having-treasure that automatically counts as laying up treasure in heaven. Peter has no treasure at all because he invested it all in a high risk get-rich-quick scheme which went bust. He may have no treasure, but his actions don't count as laying up treasure in heaven, because he lacks that trusting generosity trust that counts as faith. That is why Jesus makes it quite specific here: 'sell your possessions and give alms'.[21] It is your generosity which makes 'having-treasure-nowhere' mean the same thing as 'having-treasure-in-heaven'.

JESUS TALKING: LOVE OF GOD

Finally, here is a rather different case. To lay up treasure in heaven is to lay up treasure nowhere. To fear God is to fear nobody. But the logic works differently when we speak about love. To love God means to love *everybody*, not nobody.[22] But once again the grammar of loving God is strange, and suggests that by loving God we are not finding an object called God, identifying it and loving it, as if God were someone we could identify, locate and love. This is what it sounds like in Matthew's gospel where Jesus is asked about which is the greatest commandment. This is his reply:

> You shall love the Lord your God with all your heart and with all your soul and with all your mind. This is the great and first commandment. And a second is like it: You shall love your neighbour as yourself. From these commandments depend all the law and the prophets. (Matthew 22:37-40)

What is odd about this commandment of love? Say, for example, I love six people. And then I meet someone else and

---

[21]   So Jesus, when he is confronted by a rich young man, invites him not only to sell his possessions and give the proceeds to the poor, but also to follow him; that is to say, to start living the life that counts as being a disciple (Matthew 19:16-22).

[22]   Moore 1988, 112-15.

start to love them. Then I will love seven people. But if I love six people and also love God, that is not a seventh person *in addition to* the other six. In a sense, if I loved those six people I was already loving God.

It works the other way round too. I can perfectly logically say, 'I hate Jock, but I love Jill.' That's because Jock and Jill are two individuals, two potential objects of love. But the language of 'loving God' does not work like that. The First Letter of St John says that if we don't love our neighbour then we aren't loving God either:

> If anyone says 'I love God' and hates his brother, he is a liar; for one who does not love his brother whom he has seen cannot love God whom he has not seen. (1 John 4:20)

Clearly it is impossible to separate Christ's two-fold command of loving God and loving neighbour. In the case of two individuals I can love one and hate the other, but that is only possible in the case of two individual beings. But – and this is the great difference – I *cannot* love God without loving Jill. The logic of love, the grammar of God if you like, means that God is not an additional third individual alongside Jock and Jill. He is not another potential object of my love. My love of God can only be understood in terms of my love of Jock and Jill, and many other people.

And this helps us to understand another passage in Matthew's Gospel. We have just read the verse where Jesus says that the whole Law and the Prophets hang on love of God and love of neighbour. But in another place, he says this: 'Whatever you wish that men would do to you, do so to them; *for this is the law and the prophets*' (Matthew 7:12). In other words, that reduction of the Law to the commandment to love God and Neighbour has now apparently been reduced even further: do to others as you would be done by; that is 'love them'. There is no mention of God here at all. Presumably that's because the only thing that counts as loving God is loving your neighbour. Indeed St Paul makes exactly the same point:

> Owe no one anything except to love one another; for he who loves his neighbour has fulfilled the Law. The commandments, 'You shall not commit adultery, You shall not kill, You shall not steal, You shall not covet,' and any other commandment, are summed up in this sentence: 'You shall love your neighbour as yourself.' Love does no wrong to a neighbour; therefore love is the fulfilling of the Law. (Romans 13:8-10)[23]

Let's look at it in a somewhat more behavioural way. If someone tells you that I love Jock, and you want to see if it is true or not, you will first want to identify Jock as an individual being. And then you will watch me to see if I behave in a loving way towards him. If I seem to enjoy his company and his friendship, if I help him when he is in a fix, if I visit him when he is lonely, buy a drink for him from time to time, show him kindness, reassurance, and so on, then you will think, yes, Gilbert does love Jock. But if someone tells you that I love God, even if it is true, you will not be able to identify any being anywhere to whom I behave lovingly. If you search for an individual whose company I seek out, and for whom I do various favours, then you will miss the point. You won't find such an individual. And that's not because God is so hard to spot, being invisible. It is because the grammar of loving God doesn't involve acting lovingly towards an individual called God. It is not the same as loving Jock. In fact, if you want to know whether or not I love God, Jesus would suggest that you should watch not how I behave towards an invisible God, but how I behave towards Jock and Jill, and towards lots of other perfectly visible people.

Rather than thinking of 'loving God' as behaving in

---

[23] He makes the same point elsewhere - 'For the whole law is fulfilled in one word: 'You shall love your neighbour as yourself' (Galatians 5:14).

a certain way towards an invisible individual called 'God', because there is no such distinct individual, we might think about what it means for us to love one another. St Augustine has some interesting things to say about loving God in his *De Trinitate*, where he explores the implications of 1 John 4:7-12, which says this:

> Beloved, let us love one another; for love is of God, and he who loves is born of God and knows God. He who does not love does not know God; for God is love. In this is the love of God made manifest among us, that God sent his only Son into the world, so that we might live through him. In this is love, not that we loved God but that he loved us and sent his Son to be the expiation for our sins. Beloved, if God so loved us, we also ought to love one another. No man has ever seen God; if we love one another, God abides in us and his love is perfected in us.

Here is what Augustine says about love, often citing this passage:

> We find many other occurrences in the holy writing where only love of neighbour seems to be commanded for our perfection, while love of God is passed over in silence (though the law and the prophets depend on both commandments). But this is because if someone loves their neighbour, it follows that they must above all love love itself. But 'God is love, and whoever abides in love abides in God.' ... Let no one say, 'I don't know what to love.' Let him love his brother and let him also love that love itself. For he knows the love with which he loves better than he knows the brother whom he loves. So there! He can already know God better than he knows his brother. God is more known because more present, more known because more inward to him, more known because more sure. ... Let us

observe how much the apostle John commends brotherly love: 'Whoever loves his brother,' he says, 'remains in the light, and there is no scandal in him.' (1 John 2:10) ... But he seems to be silent about the love of God, but he would never do this unless he wanted God to be understood in terms of brotherly love. And he says it most clearly a little later in the same letter: 'Beloved, let us love one another, for love is from God, and every one who loves is born of God and knows God. Whoever does not love does not know God, for God is love.' (1 John 4:7) This passage clearly and sufficiently declares how this brotherly love (and brotherly love is the love with which we love each other) is proclaimed on the highest authority not only to be *from* God, but actually to *be* God (*De Trinitate* VIII, 10, 12).

JESUS TALKING: GLORY

In John's Gospel, Jesus asks, 'How can you believe, who receive glory from one another, and do not seek the glory that comes from the only God? (John 5:44). Let's pursue the same kind of pattern as in the previous examples. First of all, we must observe that generally speaking it is possible to seek glory from more than one person. I can work really hard and write a wonderful book, and so get glory from my head of department, and from my wife, from a reviewer in the *London Review of Books*, and from my dad – who always wanted me to write this book. That's four individuals I can get glory from, all at once! But if I seek glory from God, this passage implies, I *cannot* seek glory from anyone, not even my dad. This is a logical remark about the meaning of the word 'God'. He is not one of the individuals whose glory I might seek, in addition to the others who will praise and admire me. To seek glory from God is to seek glory from *nobody*, and God is the one who rewards you when *nobody* rewards you.[24]

---

[24]   Moore 1988, 140ff.

JESUS TALKING: SECRECY AND SERVICE

What we are establishing with all these examples is not more accurate 'information about God', but an understanding of a linguistic pattern, something about how God-talk works in the lives of people who talk about God. Here is another example of this linguistic pattern which we find in the way Jesus talks about God. He says:

> 'Beware of practising your piety before men in order to be seen by them; for then you will have no reward from your Father who is in heaven. Thus when you give alms, sound no trumpet before you, as the hypocrites do in the synagogues and in the streets, that they may be praised by men. Truly I say to you, they have received their reward. But when you give alms, do not let your left hand know what your right hand is doing, so that your alms be in secret; and your Father who sees in secret will reward you.' (Matthew 6:1-4)

God is the one who 'sees' you when you are acting in secret. In other words, God sees you when *no one* sees you. If you did it in front of people, publicly and seeking their praise, then effectively God would *not* see you – at least not for the purposes of 'being seen' which Jesus is talking about. To do it before God is to do it before nobody.

A little later in Matthew's gospel:

> 'No one can serve two masters; for either he will hate the one and love the other, or he will be devoted to the one and despise the other. You cannot serve both God and mammon' (Matthew 6:24).

Actually, it isn't quite true that no one can serve two masters. I serve my boss in the University of Glasgow during the day, and

79

I serve the manager of a local pub where I pull pints behind the bar at night. It may get a little complicated at times – the head of department in the university doesn't like it that I go home at five o'clock and get changed to work in the pub, instead of attending evening seminars; the manager of the pub doesn't like it that I sit at one of the tables and mark student essays after closing time. As I say, it can get complicated, but I do my best to serve both my masters and love them both. So it is actually possible to serve two masters, but that is because they are two individuals. But 'serving God' is different. In the case of serving God, the 'service' in question is of such a kind, so transformative of the 'servant', that he or she cannot serve any other master. That is not because 'serving God' takes up so much time that you don't have time to serve anyone else. It's because 'serving God' means serving no master, being free of that kind of relationship altogether.

But 'serving God' also means 'serving everyone'. As Jesus says, after assuming the role of a servant and washing his disciples' feet, 'I have given you an example, that you also should do as I have done to you' (John 13:15). As St Paul says, 'Be servants to one another' (Galatians 5:13). This does not mean we have to serve one another *in addition* to serving God. God is not an extra master *in addition* to other masters. God and other people are not a list of individuals to be added together as masters for us to serve, because God is not an individual. God cannot be a member of any list of beings.

Strangely then, the service of God means both (a) serving *no one*, so that you are completely free from all masters, and (b) serving *everyone* freely and with love. In all these cases, the language deploys pictures to excite our imagination, but the pictures continually suggest to us that God is not one of the things we have to deal with.

CHAPTER FOUR.

GOD BEING HUMAN BEING GOD: INCARNATION

THE SHOCK OF THE CANON

WE ARE GOING to move on now from the New Testament period to the next three or four centuries of the Christian era. These are the centuries when the Bible had already been written. That is to say, the texts which *now* comprise the Bible had been written. However, it wasn't entirely clear to everyone which texts should be in the Bible and which should be excluded. There were many apocryphal texts floating around in the Mediterranean world, texts that we *now* regard as apocryphal or not part of the Bible, but were regarded in the second to the fourth centuries as potentially at least part of the Bible. The canon, the official list of what was 'in', had not yet been fixed, and the decision about which books to include was really a long slow process of trial and error. And in a sense this process has still not completely finished among the Christian churches. In the sixteenth century, church reformers decided that several of the books that had hitherto been regarded as part of the Bible were not God's word after all, and out they went – at least from Protestant bibles, though Catholics and Eastern Orthodox still use them. So there is still a question among modern Christians about which books are in and which books are out. But the New Testament books were mostly settled pretty early on in this period – certainly by the fourth century – with the exception of the book of Revelation or Apocalypse, which was still being excluded in the mid-fourth century by some major figures like Cyril of Jerusalem, and as late as the seventh century in some quarters.[25]

What happens when you have a canon of scripture, a body of texts which have been defined as authoritative? One of the things it does is that it presents you with texts which are unavoidable, things you might find difficult or embarrassing, or perhaps just hard to understand. People sometimes think that the formation of a canon should be seen as a limiting thing, as if it were saying 'These are the things you have to read, and you don't have to read anything else because nothing else has any authority.' But this is not really how the canon works. The decision that these 27 books of the New Testament are all authoritative is not a narrowing and exclusive act. It's saying these 27 books are all inspired, and you have to read *at least* this much. Of course, you should read more, and you can have other ideas and inspirations. But you should *at least* read these books and treat them as inspired, and use them as a yard-stick to test other things that you read. The formation of a canon should not be seen as an attempt to create a narrow vision or to restrain readers who are naturally wide-ranging and voracious. It is rather meant to provoke people who are inclined to think their thoughts in line with the small circle of ideas which happens to be the social convention or the current wisdom of their society, and to get them to think *bigger* thoughts; and in particular to confront them with something

---

[25] It was not included in the list of Gregory of Nazianzus which was accepted at a council in Constantinople in AD 692. It was not accepted at all in the Syrian church, and as late as the sixteenth century Martin Luther suggested that this book, together with Hebrews, James ('an epistle of straw') and Jude, should be excluded from the canon of the New Testament.

that is so astonishing, so apparently mad and disturbing, that it breaks open that small circle of ideas that most of us have most of the time. In this chapter we will look at how Christians in the second, third and fourth centuries – and even in the fifth – struggled to make sense of the text that they were simply landed with. It contains difficult ideas. It contains ideas that would completely undermine some of the assumptions of their society – or for that matter our society. The presence of a canon is a way of making sure we don't get anaesthetised by conventional thinking. It calls us back again and again to the strangeness and wildness and difficulty of what early Christians thought God had done, and it prevents us from avoiding the shock of it.

Perhaps the most astonishing – even scandalous – of these ideas is the idea of the Incarnation: Jesus Christ, the human being at the centre of the New Testament who lived and walked in the Roman province of Judaea about two thousand years ago, was God. God, the eternal, has become a human being in history, being born, living, and dying a shameful and violent death. This was an idea that was, in the context of all contemporary ideas, shocking and monstrous: 'a stumbling block to Jews and foolishness to the Greeks' (1 Corinthians 1:23). The history of the first centuries of Christianity is in part the history of people trying to make sense of this appalling notion – or in some cases trying to avoid it altogether. Here are a few of the canonised New Testament passages, that these early Christians had to make sense of:

Paul's letter to the Philippians 2:6-8, written perhaps around the year 60 AD.

Though he was in the form of God,
Jesus did not count equality with God a thing to be grasped,
but emptied himself, taking the form of a servant,
being born in the likeness of men.

And being found in human form,
he became obedient unto death,
even death on a cross.

Note the continuing 'he' and 'him' that runs through this passage. There is the 'he' who was 'in the form (*morphe*) of God' and who was equal to God, and this is the same 'he' who took human form and died on a cross. This 'he' is one subject, divine and eternal, but also human and capable of suffering.

By the time John's Gospel was being written down, probably around the end of the first century, this question of Jesus being both man and God had already been reflected on, questioned, challenged, and was now being hammered out. The argument over his divinity seems to have been a bone of contention in the early Jesus movement. Many simply couldn't accept it. God was eternal, beyond this world, unchangeable, incapable of suffering, immortal. How, then, can you say that Jesus was God, given that he was in this world, that he did change, that he suffered and died? How can you say those things about God? It was tantamount to idolatry and blasphemy to worship anyone as God. But this is exactly the scandalous and difficult message that John is at such pains to promote.

In the beginning was the Word,
and the Word was with God,
and the Word was God.
He was in the beginning with God;
all things were made through him,
and without him was not anything made that was made.
... And the Word became flesh and dwelt among us,
full of grace and truth;
we have beheld his glory,
glory as of the only Son from the Father (John 1:1-5, 14).

In the same Gospel we find:

[Jesus answered them,] 'My sheep hear my voice, and I know them, and they follow me ... My Father, who has given them to me, is greater than all, and no one is able to snatch them out of the Father's hand. I and the Father are one. The Jews took up stones again to stone him. Jesus answered them, 'I have shown you many good works from the Father; for which of these do you stone me?'

The Jews answered him, 'It is not for a good work that we stone you, but for blasphemy; because you, being a man, make yourself God.'

Jesus answered them, 'Is it not written in your law, "I said to you, you are gods"? If he called them gods to whom the word of God came (and scripture cannot be broken), do you say of him whom the Father consecrated and sent into the world, "You are blaspheming", because I said I am the Son of God? If I am not doing the works of my Father, then do not believe me. But if I do them, even though you do not believe me, believe the works, that you may know and understand that the Father is in me and I am in the Father.' Again they tried to arrest him ... (John 10:27-39).

The night before he died, while talking about his own death:

'And now, Father, glorify me in thy own presence with the glory which I had with thee before the world was made' (John 17:5).

Mark's gospel, an earlier text than John's, also reflects the difficulty of early hearers of the Christian message. In Mark 2:7, Jesus forgives a man's sins, and the scribes question in their hearts, 'Why does this man speak thus? It is blasphemy! Who can forgive sins but God alone?' St Paul also expresses the astonishing idea: 'For in [Jesus] the whole fulness of the deity dwells bodily' (Colossians 2:9).

We might have cited other texts which make the same

outrageous claim, but these will suffice here. The fact that such passages were canonised meant that they were unavoidable for the early Christians; everyone had to take them seriously. But the question still arose: what did they mean? How were they to be interpreted? And people tried out various ways of making sense of these passages. Broadly speaking there were three ways of understanding such passages. One way held that Jesus was God but not really human, only appearing to have a human form which was actually an illusion. Perhaps he appeared to occupy a human body, as a kind of disguise. Perhaps the body was itself a kind of illusion, an appearance of humanity which was not real. The broad term for this position is *docetism* from Greek *dokein* 'to seem, to appear': Jesus seemed to be human, but was not really. A second view held that Jesus was truly human but not divine in the fullest sense, or he only became divine by a kind of adoption – positions which appear in various guises in the teachings of Arianism (after its teacher, Arius) and Adoptionism. A third way – the way that eventually won out as the orthodox position – stated that Jesus was fully human and fully divine.

Much of people's difficulty over the Incarnation was rooted in ideas broadly associated with the teaching of 'Gnosticism'. That is a broad term which in fact covers many different types of belief, different teachers and communities and so on, but is nevertheless an identifiable cultural and religious movement which began probably in the second century AD, though it drew on much older ideas too. One of the 'family resemblances' of the Gnostic movement was an antipathy to human bodiliness and to the materiality of creation and our place in it. The Gnostics believed that the material world was not created by God, but by some second-level deity. For Gnostics, God was spirit and goodness, and had only created spiritual beings – angels, souls, and so on. A lesser being (one they called the *demiurge*) had come along later and created bodily material things. This demiurge was a false god, sometimes even regarded as evil.

For the Gnostics, then, the idea that the eternal creator God could have united himself to a human body was unacceptable, unimaginable and rather disgusting. For them the whole point of salvation was that we should be saved *out of* our bodily lives and saved *from* the material world, and that we could be saved in this way by acquiring a certain kind of hidden knowledge (*gnosis*). Our fallenness, the great cosmic disaster which had befallen humanity, was the fact of our being bodies: we should have been spirits, but we had fallen from that state of purity into the dreadful condition of being embodied. That's why some Gnostics had a certain amount of contempt for sex: it meant that people were engaging in sensual and pleasurable bodily activity, which was bad enough in itself; but more drastically, every time a fertile couple had sex there was the danger that another person would be conceived, and another pure and beautiful spirit would therefore be trapped in the corruption of human flesh. For them, our bodiliness was the problem. Salvation was salvation *from* the body.

The existence of this way of thinking is even attested by the New Testament itself: 'Many deceivers have gone out into the world, men who will not acknowledge the coming of Jesus Christ *in the flesh*' (1 John 7). Some of these Gnostics claimed that Jesus had not really been born of a woman. Others said that he had an 'astral body', a body made of the stuff of the stars which they thought were not material in the ordinary sense, so that he only *appeared* to be a human being. Others said that the son of God occupied a human body, but it wasn't really his. It was someone else's body, and he merely wore it as a kind of disguise, but he was never the person whose body it was. Others, the Manichees for example, taught that there were two great principles in creation: good and evil. Spirit was good, but matter was evil – you can see that in this respect at least they were really a variant of Gnosticism. For them the Son of God did not suffer and did not die, but they suggested that God had sent an angel along to be crucified instead, or that the body which was crucified was not really a proper human body, or that it wasn't the body of the Son of God. All these are different ways of denying that Christ was both human and divine – by saying that he only *appeared* to be human.

If these positions denied the ordinary humanity of Jesus, the Arian position solved the 'problem' by denying his divinity. For Arius, the Son is a secondary and inferior being, a quasi-deity, standing midway between the True God or First Cause and the material creation, made or begotten by God at a certain moment in time. Before that moment he did not exist, though God did. The Son was therefore himself a creature, and it was through him that the rest of the world was created. So for Arius, Christ, was not eternal, and not really God, so when Christ suffered and died God did not. A good deal of this, like the thinking of the docetists, depends on a Platonic view of the universe in which God is the topmost element in a Great Chain of Being, stretching from the sublime, eternal uncreated One, who is pure spirit, down to the formless, meaningless, unstructured darkness of pure matter. In between those two extremes are creatures – spiritual beings like Christ, angels, and so on, and material ones which are partly form and partly matter, like people, badgers, vegetables, rocks and so on.

So, there were two broad ways of denying the Incarnation: one denies Christ's humanity and the other denies his divinity. It's also worth noticing that each of these two ways also denied that God created the world, or created humanity. Each of them keeps God permanently excluded from the world by making some other thing the creator – the demiurge for the Gnostics, or the created Son for the Arians.

It took some time for Christians to hammer out a consensus about how to talk about the Incarnation. The position finally adopted by most of them is best summed up in a statement produced by a council held in AD 451 at a place called Chalcedon (now in the modern city of Istanbul) – so the formula is usually called 'Chalcedonian'. This is how they summed up their reading of the biblical texts:

> We unanimously teach and confess one and the same Son, our Lord Jesus Christ, the same perfect in divinity and perfect in humanity, the same truly God *and* truly man composed of rational soul and body, the same one in being (*homoousios*) with the Father as to the divinity *and* one in being with us as to the humanity, like us in all things but sin. The same was begotten from the Father before the ages as to the divinity, *and* was born as to his humanity in the latter days for us and our salvation from Mary the virgin mother of God. We confess that one and the same Lord Jesus Christ, the only-begotten Son, must be acknowledged in two natures, without confusion or change, without division or separation. The distinction between the natures was never abolished by their union, but rather the character proper to each of the two natures was preserved as they came together in one person (*prosopon*) and one hypostasis. He is not split or divided into two persons, but He is one and the same only-begotten, God the Word, the Lord Jesus Christ, as formerly the prophets and later Jesus Christ himself have taught us about Him, and has been handed down to us by the Symbol of the Fathers.

They have clearly worked hard to rule out a whole range of what they see as mistaken theories. But do note here that the Council of Chalcedon did not define anything about the nature of God. They did not claim to know what God was like. The formula simply says that Jesus was God and Man, without defining what 'God' meant. It assumed that God remained a mystery, but that mysterious and unknown God was fully present in Christ. In other words, if you want to know God, look at Jesus. Then you will know God, not in the sense of acquiring various pieces of information about some being called 'God', but in the more relational sense of knowing, as we know a friend, or as we know ourselves in relation to others.

And we should also note that Chalcedon did not say anything about what Jesus was like either. For that we must look to other evidence – in particular the Gospels, but for modern students we might also consider New Testament history, archaeology, other literature of the time – and try to form our understanding of Jesus from that. But the Chalcedonian fathers wanted people to understand that forming a picture of Jesus, who is God, is the way we learn to talk about God, for Jesus 'is the image of the invisible God' (Colossians 1:15).

Now this is all a kind of back-story, a preamble to our discussion of how the idea of God as Nothing might shed light on the Incarnation. The difficulty with the idea of the Incarnation can be expressed as a difficulty in accepting that one person, Jesus, can be two things at the same time. Jesus is a man, but people also wanted to say that he was God. (Or Jesus claims to be God, but he also appears to be a man.) But if 'Jesus' is the name of an individual human being, and 'God' is the name of another individual being, how could they be one and the same? Let us reach for an analogy. 'France' is the name of one country, and 'Spain' is the name of another. They are two different entities, two members of the same category – geographically locatable countries. You can't say that one is the other. It makes no sense. One being cannot be another being. I can't say of two members of the same class, let's call them A and B, that 'A is B', this individual is that individual.

So how can I say that this individual being, Jesus, is the same individual being as that other one, God? But that is not what the Incarnation is saying. It is not saying that this man and God are two individual beings who get mysteriously joined together to form one individual being The point here is that we can't count God as an individual being at all. God is not an individual alongside any other individual. God and I are not two distinct individuals. I am a distinct individual, and because of that I am distinguishable from you, and from the furniture, and from the tree outside my window. But as we have seen God is not such a being. God is nothing. So though I can't logically say 'This individual being is that individual being', I *can* say 'This individual being is God', or 'This individual man is God'. At least, from the logical point of view I can say it – even if there are other problems with it, which we will come to in due course.

Another way of objecting to the Incarnation is similar. The philosopher John Hick (in his book *The Myth of God Incarnate*) denied that Jesus could really be both man and God because these are two exclusive categories. It is like saying a shape is both a circle and a square at the same time. But the answer to this is as indicated by Herbert McCabe:

> Circles and squares and triangles and such occupy their mutually exclusive territories in the common logical world of shapes. It is part of the meaning of a circle that it is not a square or any other shape; hence to say that something is both a circle and a square is to say that it both is and is not a circle, and this ... is to say nothing at all. Similarly being human and being, say, a sheep occupy mutually exclusive territories in the common logical world of animals. It is part of the meaning of being human that one is not a sheep. And so on. But just what or where is the common logical world that is occupied in mutual exclusion by God and man?[26]

Once we have granted that God is not a thing, and therefore that God and this particular human being are not two individual and distinct beings, we have a way open to us to explore the Incarnation in more subtle ways. The New Testament has many ways of expressing this doctrine, many *images*: those

[26] McCabe, 1987, 57-8.

Johannine examples given above, such as 'the Word was made Flesh'; or in Paul's letter to the Colossians, 'in him all the fullness of God was pleased to dwell' (1:10); or Jesus's own words, 'Before Abraham was, I am.' (John 8:58). All these seek to express a belief that Jesus was both human and divine. But what it actually means for Jesus 'to be God' is not something we can give a clear account of, simply because we don't know what it means to be God. We don't know what it means for *God* to be God. We don't know what God is like. As Thomas Aquinas says, 'In this life we do not know by the revelation of grace *what* God is, and so we are joined to him as to the unknown.'[27] Or, even more dramatically: 'This is what it is to know God: that we know that we don't know what he is.' [28] When we say the man Jesus was God, we are saying something that we do not fully understand, not because we don't understand the grammar, or the meaning of the words, but because we don't know what God is.

If it were not already strange enough to say that Jesus is God, we might also notice here that there is a long Christian tradition which speaks of the union of divine and human natures not only in Christ through his Incarnation, but in all of us. As the psalmist says, 'I have said to you, you are gods, and all you of you sons of the Most High.' (Psalm 82:6). This was the verse cited by Jesus in John's Gospel in response to those who accused him of blasphemy, 'because you, being a man, make yourself God.' In the early centuries of the Church it was held not only that Jesus was fully human and fully divine, but that all humans are called to become divine in Christ. There is a little prayer in the Catholic celebration of the Eucharist which expresses this most succinctly: when the priest puts a

[27] *Summa Theologiae* 1a, 12, xiii ad primum: 'Per revelationem gratiae in hac vita non cognoscamus de Deo quid est, et sic ei quasi ignoto coniunga-mur.'
[28] *In Librum De divinis Nominibus* cap. vii, lectio iv: 'Hoc ipsum est Deum cognoscere, quod nos scimus nos ignorare de Deo quid sit.'

little drop of water into the cup of wine he says, 'By the mystery of this water and wine, may we come to share in the divinity of Christ, who humbled himself to share in our humanity.' As Christ is divine by nature, so we are to become divine by adoption through Christ. Again, this is not a matter of one being, you, becoming another being, God – or *vice versa* This is a matter of one being, you, becoming one with the God who is *not* another being. We find the theme appearing in various early Christian writers. Irenaeus the bishop of Lyons (d. 202) wrote that 'God became what we are in order to make us what he is'. Clement of Alexandria (d. 215) said that 'the word of God became a man, so that you might learn from a man how to become God'. Athanasius (d. 373) said that 'the Son of God became man so that we might become God', and the great Augustine (d. 430) says 'if we have been made children of God, we have also been made gods'. This does not mean that God, who was once one thing, is now many things. It does not mean that one thing (you) become another thing (God). It means that just as the fulness of God was in one human being – Jesus – without any change to God, so the fulness of God can be in other human beings by grace.

SUFFERING, EVIL AND INCARNATION

One of the great challenges for Christian theology is the problem of evil. If God is the omnipotent Creator, and if he is good and loving, why do we suffer? Why are the innocent oppressed, tortured and killed? Why must parents watch their children die of hunger? This has always been a problem for Christian theology, and many are the ways in which people have tried to theorise about it. It may be that some of the appalling events of the twentieth century have served to sharpen the question for theology, in particular the *Shoah* or holocaust, the mass-murder of millions of European Jews by the Third Reich in the 1930s and 40s. There were of course other large-scale human slaughters in that century - the thirty-year genocide of the Armenians by Turkey, for example, or the murder of up to two million of his own people by Pol Pot's Khmer Rouge in 1970s Cambodia, to name but two. Perhaps these more recent catastrophes had a greater impact on our thinking, not only because technology had made industrial-scale cruelty more 'effective' (automatic weapons, poison gas, trains), but it was able to make such horrors more vividly present to a wider world through television, radio and journalism. Although mass murder has been a feature of human history for as long as we have been capable of it, Christian theologians seem to have found the *Shoah* so remarkable that it forced renewed thinking about a theology of suffering and evil. People were so shocked – perhaps because of the sheer scale of industrialised murder, perhaps because it was the people of Israel, the Jews, who were largely involved, perhaps for other reasons – that they returned again and again to the long and anguished question of the goodness of God and the existence of evil. Such suffering, and such evil, seemed to call into question the goodness of God, or the existence of God, among people of good will. It was almost as if theologians felt they had to exculpate the Creator, to find him innocent of wrongdoing.

One of the many approaches to this quest was to say, in response to the horrors of history, that God suffers with his creatures. God looks at the world he has made and sees all the suffering and cruelty of it all, the things people do to each other, and he suffers with the victims. Several modern theologians have remarked that if someone sees terrible cruelty and suffering, and doesn't at least show sympathy, doesn't suffer some sense of grief at what is going on, then they can hardly be called loving, kind or merciful. If that is so of human beings, how much more must it be true of God, who is supposed to be infinitely more loving and kind and merciful than we are. Surely, they argue, when God sees what is going on he must be grief-stricken and anguished at our cruelty, or he wouldn't be a loving God at all? If he doesn't respond to our suffering with suffering of his own, he must be callous, insensitive, indifferent, hard-hearted. God must surely be suffering alongside us.

So the argument goes. The people who suggest this way of talking about God are sometimes called 'Process Theologians', because they believe that God undergoes processes, processes of change and suffering and so on. In this picture, God created the world a very long time ago, but since then he has let it get on with its own business; and having granted us freedom to do what we want he now gazes on our history with loving care, rejoicing when we are good, suffering anguish when we are wicked. I should add that I think this is partly motivated by the desire of believers to somehow get God off the hook. For them, the holocaust and other such catastrophes leave God in the dock accused of neglect, or impotence, or not being as good as we thought he was. The 'case for the defence' for God, so to speak, is that he is just like a kind person: when he sees human suffering, he himself suffers appalling anguish and grief. So at least he's sympathetic, compassionate – and that's a kind of love, isn't it?

But the process theologian's view is entirely based on the assumption that God is an individual being. It assumes that God and the world co-exist. It has a picture in which there are all the beings which God has created and then there is another being called God, who is a kind of spectator of history, someone who is out there looking in, as if watching a great epic film, and either getting emotionally involved and weeping at the sad bits, or remaining impassive and a detached or hard-hearted spectator. But if God is not a thing, if God is not another individual being alongside the world and its creatures, then it makes no sense to say that he is a spectator looking in. Furthermore, if God is the creator of the world, he is also the creator of everything that happens in the world, because all that happens is simply part of the world. He did not set it up thousands, or millions, or billions of years ago and just allow it to get on with its own business. If God is the creator, he must be outside time – for time is itself part of creation – and therefore he cannot have done X, Y, or Z at any moment in time. He creates all kinds of things which do happen in time (the Big Bang, the Wall Street Crash, the evolution of the hedgehog), but God does not *act in time*. He does not reside within any kind of continuum – space or time or anything else. This is what is meant by the word 'eternal' – not that it goes on forever, but that it is outside time. God creates the continuum of time (and space), so he himself must act outside time. So everything that exists is created, and it is created and held in being by God's *eternal* creative activity. All that is comes from his hand. So how can anything act *on* God? How can God be affected by anything? If everything that exists exists because of God, and everything that happens happens because of God, how can anything happen *to* God?

Another way of putting it: if God is the creator of everything, including all space and all time, and is therefore outside time, outside any kind of continuity or consecutiveness, then how can we say that he changes? Change is always change from one state to another – sad yesterday, happy today; here today, gone tomorrow; hairy today, bald as a coot in five years' time. And because change involves a before and after, it can only happen *within* the order of time, and so within the order of creation. But if God is not in the order of time and creation, then he can't have any before and after, and so he can't have any change. So nothing can change him. Nothing can make him sad or happy, because either of those things implies a change.

Does this mean that God is static and insensitive as the process theologians said in the sixties and seventies? Well, it might look that way at first sight. If I say of any individual being that it doesn't change, that it is changeless, then I can also say that it is static. But it is only possible to say this of individual things which exist in time. To remain static is to remain unchanged *for a duration of time* – whether it's a second, or a day, or fourteen billion years. Therefore only individual creatures embedded in time can be static. To call a human being static or unchanging might make sense – it might even be regarded as something of a flaw in a person to be static, not to respond with happiness or sadness to what she sees around her, not to be able to grow in understanding or compassion. But if God is not an individual, and if he is not embedded in time, then he cannot be static. You can't say 'If God doesn't grieve over our suffering he must be static.' It doesn't work. It's like saying that if God isn't a Celtic supporter he must be a Rangers fan. It assumes that you have to be either one or the other. But such a choice – between 'changing' and 'static' – only applies to individuals within the created order, within the order of time. Neither change nor stasis can apply to the Creator.

Incidentally what we have said about God's timelessness can also shed light on other things we say about God, other images we have of God. For example, God cannot learn things, because learning things is also a process which is only possible for time-bound creatures. Learning things means changing from ignorance to knowledge, and there is no change in an eternal God. This has implications about what we mean when we say that God 'knows' things (including the knowledge that we suffer and die, that people can be cruel) but we'll look into that later. Likewise, in spite of the fact that we often pray using phrases such as 'Remember, O Lord', we know that God cannot actually remember in the sense that people remember, in the sense of calling to mind now what he didn't have in mind half an hour ago. He does not need reminding. He is in no danger of forgetting. And that is not because he has such a great memory. It is because remembering, forgetting, reminding and calling to mind are all things that only time-bound creatures like us can do. But God cannot, because he is not in time.

IMMANENCE – GOD WITH US

So far, we seem to have completely removed God from the world of suffering, and we have removed him from the world of compassion and sympathy, by suggesting that he is not an individual and he is not in time or space. He is simply too far beyond the existence of individual beings to be 'involved' as another individual alongside us. So, what can we say about God in relation to suffering? Is this God-as-Nothing *simply* remote, therefore? Is there no sense in which God is involved in our lives, our hopes and joys, losses and sorrows? If God were an individual existing alongside other individuals, then his lack of involvement would certainly indicate remoteness, hard-heartedness, unresponsiveness. And that would be quite against the view of God that most Christians hold. After all, we sing that 'the Lord is close to the broken-hearted; those whose spirit is crushed he will save' (Psalm 34:18). And Christians believe that in the person of Christ, God has become close to people in the most intimate way possible, by becoming one of us. He is *Immanuel,* or God-with-us. If we believe that, we must ask *how* is he close?

The idea of God as Nothing offers us a way of understanding what his closeness to us means and how he is intimately involved in this world. In the first place, he is involved as the immediate creative power upholding every being in creation. Each being, and every event, is created by God, and by virtue of this he is infinitely closer to his creatures than any individual being could be. Between any two individual beings there is always some distance, some degree of separation. But God is not another individual, but is the constant source of your being. So though there are ways in which it makes sense to talk of him as remote, as completely other, he is also intimate and close in a way which no individual being could be. As Augustine said in his *Confessions,* 'You were more inward than my inmost inward part, and higher than the highest element within me.'[29] Or as God says in the Qur'an, using a more physical image, 'We have already created man and know what his soul whispers to him, and We are closer to him than his jugular vein' (50:16). It is not possible for this kind of closeness to exist between two individual beings. It *is* possible for such closeness to exist between a person and God, because God is not another individual being, or a person.

So God is close to us by virtue of being Creator. But in the Incarnation of Christ, the Word made Flesh, there is an even more radical sense in which God engages with human suffering. In the doctrine of the Incarnation what is being said is that there is an individual being, whom we call Christ, who is both divine and human. Because we are talking of a single being here, whatever we say of Jesus the man is also true of God. There is one single 'he' who is eternal, through whom the universe was made, and who was born and lived and died in the Roman province of Judaea, two thousand years ago. There is only one subject here, who is both human and divine. And therefore we can say that God lay in a manger in a stable and that he grew up and ate and drank and celebrated with his friends; we can say that Roman soldiers spat at God and flogged him. We can say that the unchangeable eternal God who created the world experienced total failure and death. *God died. But he died as man.* God's involvement in human pain is not to sit in heaven looking at us compassionately and sadly. God's involvement in human pain is actually his own human pain – not sympathetic misery, but the pain of flogging and of nails in his hands and a spear in his side; also the pain of fear and of being abandoned by his friends. The pain is human pain, but that human pain was suffered by God. It is God's pain, because in Christ God suffered these things as man.

And what the Fathers of Chalcedon wanted us to

---

[29] *Confessiones* 3, vi. 11: *tu autem eras interior intimo meo et superior summo meo.*

understand is this: God *as God* is simply perfect unchanging joy, lacking nothing, whose overflowing love is the cause of existence. But God *as man* suffers and dies with us – *as man*. The cross of Christ is what the unchanging eternal love and joy of God looks like when it is projected onto the crooked and twisted screen of human history; it is what happens when the God who is love becomes human and places himself 'at the mercy of men who don't know the meaning of the word'.

But just as God in Christ took on *human* suffering, so in Christ a suffering humanity takes on God's eternal life and joy. And this is critical for our understanding of how God deals with human suffering. For the process theologians, who protest against the 'indifference' of a remote and static and uninvolved God, they imagine a God who sees human suffering from his heavenly throne and embraces it with his own compassionate sadness and anguish. I would want to ask if that is really a great grounds for hope? When someone is crushed by grief and despair, the process theologian implies, 'God sees your suffering and grieves for you, and he will draw you into himself, and he will embrace your suffering with his own sympathetic grief for eternity.' Is that really grounds for hope? For the Fathers of Chalcedon, God is not a sympathetic observer watching from his throne in heaven. He actually undergoes real human suffering on the very earthly throne of the cross, and embraces that suffering not with divine anguish, but with the divine joy, which is the life he shares with his friends, eternally.

CHAPTER FIVE.

GRACE AND FREEDOM

THERE HAVE ALWAYS been, you might say, two voices in Christian preaching.[30] The first voice says that what we do matters. It says that we will be judged on what we do, how we treat one another with love. It matters absolutely. As Augustine says, 'my love is my weight'.[31] Our love is what makes us what we are, gives us our meaning. Are we capable of giving ourselves in love or not? Perhaps we remember that passage from Matthew 25, where the Son of Man comes to judge the earth, and it is our care for the hungry, the naked, the sick and the prisoner which becomes the criterion of judgement. And we are called not to love in expectation of return: 'If you love those who love you, what credit is that to you? Even sinners love those who love them.' (Luke 6: 32) And so there is in Christianity a constant call to repentance, to transformation – a call to root our lives in that ground of love and mercy. If our love and knowledge of God can only be determined by how we treat each other (as we saw in Chapter 3), and in particular how we treat the powerless and the vulnerable, then it follows that salvation requires a certain kind of life: a life of virtue, of

---

[30] Márkus 2005.
[31] *Confessiones* XIII, ix: *pondus meum amor meus; eo feror, quocumque feror,* 'my weight is my love; and by it I am carried wherever it is that I am carried'.

human goodness. You could say that this first voice calls for the imitation of Christ. What we must do is do as he did. Our eternal destiny is closely connected to how we live our lives now. You might call this voice the juridical voice, since it treats Christian life under the metaphor of law and judgment. If you live like this, you'll be okay, you'll be happy forever. If you do bad, if you sin, you'll fall foul of the law, you will be judged and condemned for eternity. That's the first voice, then.

But there is a second and rather different voice in the Bible, and in Christian preaching. In this voice, this second way of thinking, although there is an exhortation to virtue and goodness, there is a recognition of human failing, weakness, sinfulness. In this scenario, we remain sinners throughout our lives, and yet *still* have some hope of salvation. This second voice recognises that we constantly struggle with our own weakness, fearfulness, selfishness, lustfulness, thirst for power or prestige, all the daft things we do out of insecurity, and the wicked things we do to hurt each other, but that these things need not necessarily separate us eternally from God. This is the second voice. It is a voice that speaks not *only* of imitating the virtue of Christ, but also of asking for the mercy of Christ when we fail. It is a voice that hates sin, that longs to be rid of sin, but also accepts that God delights in showing mercy to sinners – not merely rewarding the righteous. And not only does this voice stress that we are all sinners, and remain sinners in this life, it also stresses that we need God's help to attain virtue: we want to be good, to act justly and mercifully, but we fail again and again We are easily tempted. In this voice we hear a call not just to righteousness and to moral perfection, but also to humility – you need to be humble enough not to rely entirely on your own strength, but to pray, to ask God for help and strength. It is a voice which is not so much juridical as therapeutic, admitting brokenness and failure, and seeking healing.

I should add, of course, that both of these voices, speak

about God in metaphors, using the picture of a relationship between two individual beings. The first voice paints a picture in which one individual learns what the other has done and responds with judgement. As we have seen God is outside time, and cannot undergo changes – he cannot 'learn' anything, nor can he 'respond' with reward or punishment. Only another individual being alongside us in time and space can do those things. The judicial image nevertheless works as a picture, and makes sense. When we come before a judge there is a connection between what we have done and what is going to happen to us – there is a connection between my having burgled all my neighbours and my going to jail. So the Gospel wants to say that there is a connection between what we do and what becomes of us: the love with which we love each other today is the love which defines our eternal destiny. And a judicial metaphor seems to work – to some extent at least – in this voice.

Similarly with the second voice, the therapeutic voice, we also use pictures to express it which are in terms of relationship. The therapeutic voice suggests that there are two individual beings involved: a needy one and a therapist; one who is constantly in need of help, and one who is constantly on hand to provide that help if only we will ask. Of course, this is only a picture too, as God can't respond to anything. He can't respond to being asked for help. In fact, if we ever ask for help that is because God has already created that longing prayer in us. Remember, St Paul says that our prayer is, even before we have thought of it, 'the Holy Spirit crying out in our hearts, Abba! Father!' (Galatians 4:6; Romans 8:15). This second therapeutic, healing voice is therefore as much a picture as the first judicial voice.

Now in the early fifth century, a dispute arose in the Church over these two voices, and how they related to each other. We're going to look now at the thought of St Augustine in this dispute, and why some people opposed him. Augustine was a convert to Christianity, having been a Manichean in the early years of his life (the Manicheans were one of the groups we looked at in Chapter 4 who saw the existence of the material world as a catastrophe, and our own bodiliness as the source of all human evil). Augustine enjoyed a great reputation in the Roman world as a scholar and an orator, but he abandoned this rather glorious career, and more importantly he abandoned his Manichean ideas. It is very important to remember Augustine's early involvement in this theory, and his subsequent absolute rejection of it. He was quite clear in his later life about what he had believed as a young man, and equally clear about his rejection of it. When he became a Christian under the influence of Ambrose of Milan, Augustine rejected the Manichean idea that God made some good things (which were not physical) and that an evil demiurge had made the physical world. He came to accept that God made everything, and that everything is good – every being, spiritual and material, visible and invisible, everything that exists is *good*. This is fundamental to Augustine's thought, and it will be important to bear this in mind as we look at his views. Here is what he says in the *Confessions*:

> Hence I saw and it was made clear to me that you made all things good, and there are absolutely no substances which you did not make. As you did not make all things equal, all things are good in the sense that taken individually they are good, and all things taken together are very good. For our God has made all things very good (*Confessions* VII, 18).

So Augustine became a Christian. In his early years he was hopeful, even optimistic, about his new life, imagining that by living peacefully with like-minded friends in a kind of gentlemen's retreat, meditating on scripture, he would grow in perfection and holiness and perhaps leave behind the sinfulness of 'the world'. But he soon found that his optimism was unjustified. He found that he still suffered from temptations to sin – he was selfish, had moments of vanity and pride (and for him pride was the worst of all sins). He found that his sensual nature still tempted him not just to take a proper enjoyment in bodily pleasures, but to exceed that enjoyment, to lust after such pleasures. In other words, he found that conversion to Christianity had not been a sudden and total cure for all his sinfulness.

And so he began to pray for God's help in becoming good. There is one passage where he describes his conversion – 'I tasted you, and now I feel only hunger and thirst for you. You touched me, and now I am set on fire to attain the peace which is yours.'[32] But in spite of this longing, he goes on to say, 'for the present I am *not* full of you, and therefore I am a burden to myself'. And he makes this claim on God:

> My entire hope is in your very great mercy. Grant what you command, and command what you will.[33]

And this was the passage that got Augustine into trouble. There was a certain Roman lawyer called Pelagius, a British scholar who had gone to Rome in the late fourth century and become a lawyer. He had also turned into a very strict Christian moralist, and was the guide of several upper-class Roman Christians in their villas, and was demanding the highest moral standards from all his followers. When he read Augustine's *Confessions*, and in particular this passage, he was outraged. According to Augustine:

> I said to our God, and said it often, 'Grant what you command, and command what you will.' These words of mine Pelagius of Rome could not stand when they were recalled in his presence by a certain brother and fellow-

---

[32] Confessiones, 10, xxvii (38), p. 201.
[33] *ibid*, xxix (40) 202.

bishop of mine; and contradicting them somewhat excitedly, he nearly sued him who had mentioned them.[34]

What was Pelagius so upset about? Well remember he was a lawyer. His image of Christian life was essentially a legal one. He lived by that first voice we talked about at the beginning, the voice of commandment, reward and punishment. For Pelagius, we had been given the law and we knew what to do. We just had to make up our minds to do it, and then get the reward – or else fail to do it and be punished. We didn't need God's help, because we were free. A Christian was an adult, he said, and responsible for himself or herself. Or as his disciple Julian expressed it, *homo libero arbitrio emancipatus a deo* - 'by free will, a man is set free from God'. Decide what to do and do it! And if you do it, you can call yourself a Christian. If you don't do it, as far as Pelagius was concerned you weren't a Christian at all, and there was no place in the Church for you, and there was no place in God's kingdom for you either. And this was true of all of God's commandments. For Pelagius there was no commandment more important than any other. Commandments were only important because they were God's commandments, not because of any intrinsic merit of their own. So getting a little drunk was just as evil as committing murder, because both of them were forbidden by God. And if you did either there would be no eternal happiness for you.

Now Augustine was not a lawyer, and his theology betrays little of the lawyer's mindset. A lawyer is concerned to establish guilt or innocence, and to arrange for the proper punishment of the guilty. That is the picture which shapes his or her worldview, at least professionally. But I think that one of the most important facts about Augustine is that after his early time as a kind of secluded scholar living in a north-Italian villa

---

[34]   *De Dono Perseveramtiae* XX, 53 [PL 45, 1026].

with other like-minded gentlemen, he became the bishop of a North-African town, a place called Hippo – now called Annaba, a town in modern Algeria. Hippo was a Mediterranean port full of traders, workers, off-duty sailors, dodgy shopkeepers, prostitutes, and perhaps some rather mediocre Christians who were not always generous in giving alms, and were sometimes tempted by pagan festivals and the glitter of consumer goods. These were the people that Augustine was responsible for as their pastor. These were the people to whom he preached, week in and week out, encouraging them to follow Christ, trying to help them understand the Gospel, and knowing that like him they were weak, constantly failing even when they *wanted* to do better. His role was not to convict the guilty, but to heal the damaged. It was for him a therapeutic role. He says in one of his books that when people sin, they often do so very much against their wills:

> Many sins are committed through pride, but not everything done wrongly is done proudly; some sins are surely committed by the ignorant, some by the weak, and for the most part by those who weep and groan while they sin.[35]

Pelagius, when faced with sinners, knew only judgement. Augustine, faced with the same sinners, while not condoning the sin, was grief-stricken and compassionate. He recognised the weakness of human will. He read and recognised in himself what St Paul said:

> I do not understand my own actions. For I do not do what I want, but I do the very thing I hate ... I do not do the good that I want, but I do the evil which I do not want. (Romans 7:15, 19)

---

[35] *De natura et gratia*, cap xxix (33).

Augustine acknowledges with Paul that even when he wants to do good, he keeps finding himself doing something else. His will is not fully under his control:

> If I tore my hair, if I struck my forehead, if I wrapped my fingers round my knees, I did it because I willed to do it. ... Yet I was not doing the things that I longed to do far more than these, and I *could* have done them as soon as I willed.[36]

This is why he turns to God in prayer and says, 'Grant what you command and command what you will' – the phrase which caused such great offence to Pelagius. It is because Augustine's own will is so conflicted and confused that he keeps failing to do what he wants to do, he keeps sinning even though he wants to stop. This is the contrast, then. For Pelagius the Christian life is lived by the obedient and the perfect; for Augustine there are plenty of mediocre Christians who fail repeatedly but are still Christians. They seek God, they long for God, but throughout their lives they fall and rise, and fall and rise again.

For Pelagius, all you have to do is to keep the law and follow the example of Christ; and you know you can because you have free will, so it is entirely up to you. For Augustine, you should certainly try as hard as you can to keep the law and follow Christ's example by living well, but it is not the end of the world if you fail, because your very failure will teach you humility, and you will ask God for forgiveness and you will ask God for help.

For Pelagius, the church was composed of those who kept the whole law of God in all its detail, without compromise, and for anyone else there was no hope.[37] For Augustine, the church

---

[36] *Confessiones* 8, vii (20).

[37] 'A Christian is one who never lies, never curses, who does not take any oath, nor return evil for evil ... in sum, who after the washing of baptism is free from sin' (Rees 1991, 150). 'The righteous prophet hates sinners, adulterers and unrighteous men and those who scorn God's commandments ... we must not even break bread with sinners' (Rees 1991, 116).

was composed of saints and sinners; it had to embrace those who were failures, who were weak-willed and wandering, because for him the Church was a place of healing, a place of encounter with Christ in prayer, in the sacraments, in the preaching of their bishop – so that imperfect Christians might slowly and painfully become more loving, more generous, more just, more merciful. It is interesting here to note Augustine's interpretation of the parable of the Good Samaritan (Luke 10: 25-37). He sees in the Samaritan the figure of Christ who comes to pick up this wounded humanity, and he sees the Church as the 'inn' where the wounds might be healed and for which the Samaritan-Christ has paid the bill.

For Pelagius, prayer was only for the person who was morally perfect. When a person prays, he says, he should be able to say:

> 'You know, Lord, how holy, how blameless, how free of all deceit and injury and plunder are the hands I stretch out to you; how righteous, how unspotted and how free from all lying are the lips with which I pour forth my prayers to you.'[38]

For Augustine, by contrast, the ideal prayer is one of the sinner who recognises his or her own failings:

> Much praying is a prolonged and loving beating of the heart in fervour towards Him to whom we pray. Usually this is an affair of sighing rather than talking, weeping more than addressing Him.[39]

---

[38] *De Vita Christiana*, 11.2 (Rees, 119). It's worth bearing in mind Christ's parable in Luke 18, where the Pharisee 'stood and prayed thus with himself: "God, I thank you that I am not like other men, extortioners, unjust, adulterers, or even like this tax collector. I fast twice a week, I give tithes of all that I get ...."

[39] *Epistola* 130, x [PL 33.502].

Again, for Pelagius, 'God does not love evil people, he does not love sinners. Whoever does evil is God's enemy.'[40] God does not love sinners! If you are a sinner and you want God to love you, all you have to do is stop sinning and obey God's commandments. Then God will love you, and you will have *earned* his love. For Augustine on the other hand, God *does* love sinners, and he calls them to repentance, he provokes them to sorrow and he strengthens them to return to love. He helps them to return precisely because he *already* loves them, even while they are sinners.[41] They don't have to *earn* his love. This help which God gives to falling and failing human beings is what Augustine calls *gratia*, 'grace'. Pelagius thought God helped people by giving them the Law to obey, and the example of Christ to imitate, together with the offer of reward and the threat of punishment. But those were an external help. For Augustine, God's help or grace is internal, a power 'poured into our hearts'. It was a grace which actively transformed the person to whom it was given.

So much for the contrast between these two views, then. And it was Augustine's line of argument, with some modifications, that won the day with the Church at large. Where Pelagius could accept only the first voice, the juridical one, the voice of law, crime and punishment, the church insisted that the second voice was *also* important, that left on our own with our conflicted wills, our weakness and disorderly desires, we would never be saved; but with God's grace helping us, strengthening and guiding us as an active inner force in our lives, then we could be raised up to goodness, to love and justice and mercy.

GOD AND FREEDOM

But how does the idea of God as Nothing come into all this? How does this idea help us to think about Augustine and his dispute with Pelagius? It is in the idea of grace. Pelagius says we

[40]   Rees 1991, 117.
[41]   Consider Romans 5:6-8.

are free, even 'free from God', and we alone are responsible for the way we use our freedom. Augustine also says we are free and responsible, but that we are free *in* God, because of God. Without God's grace, without his continuing action within us, our freedom only leads us into sin because we make such a mess of everything. In that case, Pelagius objects, how are we free? How can we be called 'free' if our unaided freedom only leads us to disaster? What is our freedom like? What is our freedom freedom *from*?

Let us think a bit about freedom. I am taking it for granted that we are talking about human freedom here. To accept Augustine's position, you really need to accept two statements as being true, even though they seem on the surface to be contradictory.[42] The first statement is implicit in the idea that God is the creator of all that exists. Everything owes its existence to God. If that is so, God must be the creator not only of individual objects in the universe, but also the creator of what they *do*. Since any particular action exists, when it might not have existed, we can say that actions are also created by God. That's the first statement. The second statement is this: that my actions are free. And this is what seems to be the crux of the problem. How is it possible for my actions to be created by God and at the same time authentically my own free actions? How can I say, as I want to, that God brings about my free actions? Surely they are *either* my free actions, *or* they are created by God? How can they be both?

Let's deal first of all with a couple of red herrings. First, we should note that there are people who claim that none of our actions are free in any real sense. We may *feel* as if we are acting freely, making free choices and judgements, but in fact all our actions, choices and judgements are determined quite mechanically by a mixture of our genetic makeup, various past influences on us (our family and friends, the conditioning

---

[42]   In what follows, I am heavily indebted to Herbert McCabe, especially his essay 'Freedom' (1987, 11-21).

of the media, and so on), and various other natural forces around us such as the weather at any given moment. For these philosophers, sometimes called 'hard determinists', none of our actions are really free, because they are simply the outcome of all these external influences. I don't happen to believe this position. But if I did, of course, there would be no theological problem about God causing 'free human acts', because there are no free human acts for such hard determinists. There is only a theological problem if I think my actions are free *and* created by God.

Another position says that an action can be free even if it *is* determined by something else – my genes for example, my upbringing or neuro-physiology. My actions may be caused by these things, but if I do them freely – that is at least without external coercion – then they are at the same time caused and free. People who think like this ('soft determinists' or 'compatibilists') are often thinking: we don't hold someone responsible for things that they do if they are forced (someone is threatening their children), or if they have been drugged or hypnotised. The soft determinist thinks that some things we do are forced or coerced, while other things that we do are 'caused' by something else *non*-coercively, and that even though they are caused by something other than our will we are still doing them freely. This seems to me to rather reduce the meaning of the word 'freedom': in what sense am I free to do or not to do something which is in fact caused by my genes? And in any case, just as with the hard determinist, if the soft determinist thinks my actions may be free *and* caused by something else, there would once again be no problem with God being the creator of my free acts.

But I take the view that a free act is one of which I am the cause, not one which is determined or caused by something other than me. My acts are my own free acts precisely because they are not caused by anything else. They are my acts, and they are free because they are determined by my reasons for doing them. If my action is free, you can say why I did it, and 'why I did it' will be an account of my reasons for doing it – what I was hoping to achieve, what I was taking into consideration, what risks I thought were worthwhile and so on. These are what determined my free action –and they involve things that constitute me in some sense such as my memory, my desire, my self-understanding, my intelligence. So you might be able to tell from my action what I loved, and what I knew. The fact that my action was caused doesn't mean it was unfree. It means rather that my free action *is* caused by something: it is caused by me and my reasons for doing it. And that is to say that I wasn't being controlled by drink or drugs, or some combination of genetic and environmental factors, and that I wasn't manipulated or hypnotised into doing it.

I should add here that I'm not suggesting that my actions are completely *un*influenced by other things – my genes, my upbringing, my education, the newspaper I read, and so on. I am to some extent conditioned by all these things and many others. Nevertheless, within this conditioning environment, I still have a power of spontaneity, choice, creativeness, that comes from me and not from anything outside of me, and to that extent I am free, and act for my own reasons, because of the stories I am telling myself about who I am and what I want.

So, to get back to our two apparently contradictory statements – first, my actions are free because they are caused by me and not by any other being. And second, God is the cause of every being and every action in creation, including my free actions. How are these compatible? Well, if you are getting the hang of my methodology by now, you will be able to see where I am going. My actions are free because they are not caused by anyone else, but God is still the cause of my free actions because God is not 'anyone else'. My free actions are free of all external interference, and God creates them because God is not external to me. God is, as St Augustine says, 'closer to me than I am to myself'.[43] If I were to say *something else* caused my action, then this would count as a denial of responsibility, a claim that I did not do it freely. But if I say God created this action, it does not count as a denial of responsibility, because God is not 'something else'. God is Nothing. My actions are free when I cause them, and apart from me nothing causes them. We can say that God creates them, but God is not another thing apart from me. God and I are not two individuals, two causes of action – we are not two of anything.

So I would argue that there is only an *apparent* difficulty in Augustine's position. He says that my good free acts are created in me by God, and without God's grace my will might choose lesser goods, reeling in confusion between one attraction and another. But my free acts are not free because I am free *from* God. They are free because I am free *in* God, or because of God. Without God there would be no freedom in my actions – indeed there would be no actions at all.

When I am a child, I am not entirely free. I rely greatly on my parents to make decisions for me, and am not held to be responsible for all my actions. But as I get older, I become more autonomous from my parents. If they are good parents they will encourage this; they will withdraw their influence from me to some extent as I find my own freedom and independence. But my parents are other people. They are existing individual beings alongside me. God is not an existing individual being alongside me, however, even though I might want to call him 'Father' or 'Mother'. If God is not an individual being of any sort, then I don't need to worry about becoming independent of him. I may become free by being independent of my parents. But if I become independent of God, I don't become free. I cease to exist, because my very existence in every moment of my life, and in every movement of my mind and my body, is created by God. Independence of God is not freedom; it is

43   *Confessiones*, 3, vi (11) p. 43.

extinction. We are not free because we move away from God, 'emancipated from God' as Pelagius believed, but precisely because God is present to us as Creator.

Of course, we have ways of talking about God which make him *sound* like another person, an individual being alongside us – but these are only images. We need to use images and, however hard we try, we cannot help picturing God as an individual existent, even an individual person, alongside us. But we should not let the images confuse or deceive us. Remember Wittgenstein: 'A picture held us captive. And we could not get outside it, for it lay in our language and language seemed to repeat it to us inexorably' (1958, §115). We have to keep thinking clearly as well. And it seems to me that if we remember that God is Nothing, then we can make sense of the resolution of that fifth-century debate about grace and freedom. For Augustine, the grace of God causes my good actions, and yet they remain fully my own actions, and fully free. And that can only be because God is Nothing.

CHAPTER SIX.

PSEUDO-DIONYSIUS: TWO WAYS OF TALKING

IN THE NEW Testament, after the resurrection and ascension of Christ, when the apostles are preaching all round the eastern Mediterranean, we find St Paul turning up in Athens, and preaching about Christ in the Areopagus, the meeting-place of the judicial and legislative council of Athens, the ruling men of the city-state. He tells these men that he has noticed lots of gods being worshipped in Athens:

> 'Men of Athens, I perceive that in every way you are very religious. For as I passed along and observed the objects of your worship, I found an altar with the inscription "To an unknown God". What therefore you worship as unknown, this I proclaim to you. The God who made the world and everything in it, being Lord of heaven and earth ... "in him we live and move and have our being", as even some of your poets have said ...' (Acts 17:22-8)

And he goes on to say that this 'unknown God', the Lord of heaven and earth, is the one who has made himself known in Jesus whom he raised from the dead. And he states that God has fixed a day on which he will raise all the dead and they will be judged by this man. Many of the Athenians mocked him when they heard of the resurrection of the dead, but some believed what he was saying, and joined him. Among them was a man known as Dionysius 'the Areopagite' – that is to say, a member of the ruling council or *areopagus*.

That is who the original Dionysius was, perhaps around 60 or 70 AD, at a moment of encounter between Greek philosophical ideas about gods and the Jewish idea of monotheism, the Creator who has now made himself known in Christ. But the writer we are going to look at in this chapter was writing more than 400 years later. He (we suppose it was a 'he') wrote in the *persona* of Dionysius the Areopagite, but he was probably writing in the fifth or early-sixth century – we don't know exactly when. It was quite a common practice in the ancient world to write under the assumed name of a great person or an admired author, and this is what our writer did. Not only did he write in the name of the first-century Dionysius the Areopagite, but he wrote his works as if they were letters addressed to the apostles and other New Testament figures of the first century. Perhaps he was hoping to give his own work more authority in this way, by associating it with great figures of the past. Or perhaps on the contrary it was an exercise in humility, refusing to seek fame under his own name or to construct an intellectual monument to himself. But more pointedly it may have been a dramatic way of identifying himself with the ideas of a person he admired. He may have adopted the name of Dionysius not to pull the wool over people's eyes, but to identify himself with the original Dionysius who was particularly known for his devotion to the 'unknown god' – since it is precisely the unknown-ness of God that our writer is going to commit himself to talking about. He was connecting the 'unknown god' of the ancient Greeks of Athens to the Jewish and Christian notion of a Creator, the God Jesus called 'Father'.

That is why he wrote under this name, and why he is now known as *Pseudo*-Dionysius.

We should also note that he wasn't entirely consistent in adopting a first-century *persona*: for one thing he cites the works of an author who was his own near-contemporary, Proclus, who died in AD 485. This would have been a bit of a give-away; any alert reader would surely have realised that he was citing such recent thinkers. Perhaps he was deliberately blowing his own cover, revealing to his readers that far from being the original Dionysius he was actually a contemporary of theirs, but also nailing his colours to the mast and declaring himself to be a disciple of the original Dionysius. Apart from his few writings we know nothing else about him. We don't even know his real name – we'll just call him Denys for short in this chapter, which is the usual English version of his adopted name. We can't be sure where he came from or where he was writing, though a lot of his work seems to point to a Syrian context.

The Church continued to preserve and value Denys' works for several centuries, even though there are one or two places in his writings where he teaches ideas that were suspect.[44] Pope Gregory the Great cited him in the late-sixth century, and the Irish scholar, John Scottus Eriugena translated him into Latin for the French king Charles the Bald in the ninth century. He would eventually have a profound influence, also, on Thomas Aquinas in the thirteenth century, especially in relation to the issues discussed in this chapter.

THE PLATONIC VISION

Like most of his contemporaries, Denys was steeped in the Platonic, or Neo-Platonic view of the Universe. The philosopher Proclus, mentioned above, was one of the most

---

[44] At one point, for example, he suggests that only good and holy priests can effectively administer the sacraments, a position akin to Donatism.

important exponents of this Neo-Platonic view at the time, and his influence on Denys is significant. It is a view of a world which is organised in a great hierarchy of being, or a chain of being, running down from the eternal and unchanging One, the Source of all being, shining its light down in beams which penetrate the darkness of matter. And out of these beams of light, individual beings appear. The universe is multi-storeyed, composed of countless layers of reality and existence, with the One causing everything beneath by pouring out 'one-ness' and 'being' through a descending sequence of intermediaries.

For Neo-Platonists the *idea* of something was more real than the thing itself. This is rather the reverse of our modern way of thinking. For most modern people a sheep is real, and the idea of a sheep is something derivative, an abstraction, so less real. But for the Neo-Platonist the idea of a sheep is much more real, because it is ultimately an idea derived from the mind of the One, and as the One pours forth its ideas they create sheep and other things in the world. The actual sheep is lower down in the chain of being than the idea that created it. The idea of a sheep is more real, because as an idea it is eternal, not subject to decay or change or fragmentation. The actual sheep standing on a hillside is less real because it is finite, changeable, and eventually someone is going to eat it.

This Platonic scheme of the cosmos is not a particularly Christian way of seeing things. It isn't something that Christians introduced; it was simply the philosophical air that people breathed in the ancient world, air that the first Christians found themselves living in and breathing too. It was what the world looked like to men and women who lived in that world, taken for granted, much as we take for granted the existence of bacteria, or the fact that the earth goes round the sun.

There are, however, problems with this Neo-Platonic scheme when Christians (or other monotheists) use it to think about God. One of the problems was that for Proclus and those who thought like him, the One which was before all being gave rise to *henads* which were the actual causes of being in the world. Each *henad* stood at the top of a chain of being which made different kinds of thing exist, and each of these *henads* was identifiable with one of the Greek gods. One of Proclus' important works was called *The Platonic Theology*, and the gods he was theologising about were these *henads* from which the existing things of the world would emerge. Clearly a Christian or other monotheist who sees the whole world as created by one God might have difficulty with a whole crowd of gods who stand between the Creator and the world.

Another way of expressing the same problem is that the Neo-Platonic view sees some things as closer to God and other things as further away. If God is at the top of a great chain of being, then the higher things are closer to him than the lower things. Angels are closer to God than humans, and humans are closer to him than sheep, and sheep are closer than rocks. It also makes much of the image of overflowing in the process of creation. The One has life and light so abundantly that they overflow and begin to flow downhill, down the slope of being. So the One's overflow creates the beings immediately below him, and then they overflow and cause the next rank, and they overflow and bring about lower creatures - people, then lower beings. In other words, it's a picture where God is not simply the immediate creator of everything, but the topmost element in a long chain of things, each of them overflowing to create the lower elements.[45]

Now the biblical tradition – the Jewish and Christian vision – seems to offer a very different view of creation in

---

[45] This would mean that God was one cause amongst other causes, albeit the first one. But as we have seen, the Creator God cannot be one member of any category of being, because categories of beings are all creatures created by him. It is perhaps dealing with this difficulty that Denys writes, 'he transcends every source, including the 'divinity' and 'goodness' spoken of here [as the source of divinity and goodness in creatures]. In other words, you may have an idea that there is a topmost source in the great chain of being, but that topmost source is not God, for 'he transcends every source', even the topmost. (Luibheid 1987, 263).

which God is the creator of each and every thing, without the need for mediating beings. Every being, in every moment of its existence, is created. God wills and knows each thing into being *directly*, not by some overflowing down the various channels and vessels of lower beings. And God is immanent, immediately present, to every being that he has created.

Denys sought to adapt the view of the philosophers: the streams of being, or the beams of light, that come pouring down on us from above, not only create us as creatures. They also enlighten us and call us back to our source. In this picture the One, or God, via intermediaries such as angels, shines on creatures and summons them back to himself, drawing us back up the chain of being, the gradient of reality, purifying us, making us more real, more luminous. Again, this is a picture which adopts the contemporary Greek imagery of being, but it's not easy to tie it into the biblical picture of human beings created directly by God, sustained by God, and returning to God in the resurrection.

But our present chapter is not about the difficulties of reconciling Neo-Platonism with biblical Christianity. The important thing for our purposes in exploring the idea of 'God as Nothing' is what Denys said about the way we *talk* about God, what we can know.

TWO WAYS OF TALKING

I want to look in particular at two works by Denys. The first is called *The Divine Names*; the second is called *The Mystical Theology*. At first sight they seem to have opposite purposes. The first work, *The Divine Names*, looks like an attempt to show that there are names which we can apply to God (many of them drawn from the Bible) which tell us something about God. The second work, the *Mystical Theology*, appears at first sight to be saying the opposite: here he pursues a line of denial. God is not like this, God is not like that, and so on.[46]

---

[46] There are actually elements of both in each of the two works mentioned, so this is a bit of an over-simplification.

There are two technical words for these two ways of doing theology or talking about God. The way of talking which makes affirmations about God, which gives names to God, and which *appears* to offer descriptions of God, is called 'cataphatic', making positive or affirmative statements. The other way, which is sometimes called 'apophatic', is the way of negation; it is a way of talking about God which seeks understanding by denying things about God, stressing how unknowable he is, how beyond speech or description or understanding.

AFFIRMATION COLLAPSES

As I say, these two ways of talking may look as if they are at odds with each other, but for Denys they are actually two ways of doing the same thing. He starts off with the assumption that God is completely unknowable (remember 'the altar to the unknown God' in Acts) and of course it follows from this unknowability that very little can be said about God at all. Or rather, since Christians actually have a great many things to say about God, he seeks to show that even though we have a lot to say, we don't have much idea what it means when we say it. He is cautious from the outset, and he admits: 'We must not dare to resort to words or conceptions concerning the hidden divinity (i.e. God), apart from what the sacred scriptures have divinely revealed'.[47] In other words, whatever words the Bible uses for God it is legitimate for Christians to use too. And by using these words we are drawn towards God. Note that he is *not* saying that these words are descriptions of God, even if they are in the Bible, nor that we know more about God as a result of using them. He is saying that by the very act of using such words *we* are transformed and are drawn towards God; we take flight in holiness; we are enlightened, and the often-obscured image of God which is within us is restored to clarity. He lists some of the names by which God 'the Cause'

[47] Luibheid 1987, 49.

(or Creator) is known, which he says are 'drawn from all the things which are caused':

> good, beautiful, wise, beloved, God of gods, Lord of lords, Holy of holies, eternal, existent ... wisdom, mind, knower ... that he is above all being, that he is sun, star, fire, water, wind and dew, cloud, stone and rock, that he is all, that he is no thing.[48]

Those last two 'names' – 'he is all, he is no thing' – are interesting. They are two names of God, but they seem to be opposites of each other. We will come back to that shortly.

Even in his most affirmative or cataphatic moments, Denys is always aware that the God about whom he says so much still remains the Unknown. His verbosity about God is almost a kind of anarchy. It uses metaphors, similes and analogies; it uses images borrowed from science, warfare, law, agriculture, sex, play, physiology and much more. He delights in all this cataphatic language - words and images which *look* descriptive, that *might* seduce the unwary mind into thinking it knows what God is like. But his method actually does the opposite.

Because we want to talk about the unspeakable God, we cannot remain silent but pile up more and more images on top of each other. But over and over again Denys reminds us, 'This is not what God is actually like'. The point of this multiplication of words or names is not to give us more and more accurate pictures of God. If I give you descriptive terms about a person, each one should normally add to your knowledge about that person. If I tell you that someone is tall, elderly, female, French – that's four bits of information, each one adding an extra element to the picture you have of the person, making it more and more precise. But that is not how Denys multiplies his names. The

---

48   Luibheid 1987, 55-6.

names don't work by giving us ever more precise descriptions of someone or something. He talks of God as light, for example – an image that he takes from the Bible, but one which also ties in very well to the Neo-Platonic scheme of things:

> The Good [i.e. God] is described as the light of the mind because it illuminates the mind of every supra-celestial being (angels) with the light of the mind, and because it drives from [human] souls the ignorance and the error squatting there. It gives them all a share of sacred light. It clears away the fog of ignorance from the eyes of the mind and it stirs and unwraps those covered over by the burden of darkness .... always urging them onward and upward as their capacity permits. So then, the Good which is above all light is given the name 'light of the mind', 'beam and spring', 'overflowing radiance'.[49]

Well, that's fairly positive language about God, using the image of light. But note that the word 'light' is used of God not to tell us what God is like, but to tell us about his effects on angels and ignorant people – it is called 'light' because it gives *us* knowledge, scattering the darkness of *our* ignorance. And then immediately after saying that we can call God 'light' he adds that God is 'above all light'. Even here, the question arises if it is *above* all light, how can it actually *be* a light? Denys gives other reasons why we might want to call God 'light': sunlight shines on things which are capable of receiving or reflecting its light; it shines throughout the world; it keeps things alive and causes them to grow; it purifies things.[50] For these reasons 'light' may be seen as a suitable name for God, but it tells us not about God in himself, but about God's *effects* in the world; not about the nature of God but about the nature of *things which depend on God*.

49 Luibheid, 1987, 75-6.
50 Luibheid, 1987, 74.

Denys also has another image for God, a little bit later, when he talks about Moses climbing Mount Sinai:

[Moses] hears the many-voiced trumpets. He sees the many lights, pure and with rays streaming abundantly. Then ... he pushes ahead to the summit of the divine ascents. And yet he does not meet God himself, but contemplates him, not him who is invisible, but rather where he dwells. This means, I suppose, that the holiest and highest of the things perceived with the eye of the body or of the mind are but the rationale which presupposes all that lies below the Transcendent One. Through them, however, his unimaginable presence is shown, walking the heights of those holy places to which the mind at least can rise. But then he [Moses] breaks free of them, away from what sees and is seen, and he plunges into the truly mysterious *darkness of unknowing*. Here, renouncing all that the mind may conceive, wrapped entirely in the intangible and the invisible, he belongs completely to him who is beyond everything.[51]

Denys understands the story of Moses in Exodus as a kind of allegory of Neo-Platonic thinking. Where Moses climbs up this mountain to receive God's law, we understand that he is climbing higher and higher on the chain of being, ascending the beams of light by which God illumines the world. What is striking, though, is that when he gets to the top of the mountain, he sees amazing lights – but these are not God. They are the holiest and highest things which lie just below God, the Transcendent One; they are brilliant lights. But when he takes that final step, when he plunges into God, he plunges into 'the truly mysterious darkness of unknowing.' Not light at all. And his knowledge is no longer the knowledge of something, but

---

[51]   Luibheid, 1987, 137.

the knowledge of Nothing. So Denys continues: 'Here, being neither oneself nor someone else, one is supremely united by a completely unknowing inactivity of all knowledge, and knows beyond the mind by knowing *nothing*'.

So even here, in the work where Denys is supposed to be giving us affirmative language about God, he is not actually telling us anything about God in himself, because God in himself is unknowable and 'beyond everything'. The point of his mountain of affirmations about God is that they are self-contradictory images. So we can call God 'light' if we want to, but Denys says we can also call him 'truly mysterious darkness'. He calls him 'brilliant darkness', and also 'dark brilliance'.[52] The contradictions are not just clever language-games; they are for Denys the natural result of talking about God. God is light. And God is also darkness. One looks like the negation of the other. Then he joins them together. God is brilliant darkness. This is not a third descriptive utterance, in addition to the first two, in good linguistic order. It is the collapse of linguistic order, which is for Denys the perfectly proper outcome of theological language when you stretch it as far as it will go, when you try to apply it carefully, and then stretch it a little further – beyond breaking point. The point of all these verbose affirmations is to demonstrate that language itself breaks down in the presence of the mystery of God, when you try talk about what God is. This is Denys's strategy here. What looks like cataphatic theology, a descriptive statement about God, turns out to be the collapse of description. An elaborate fiesta of words which *look* as if they are trying to give information about God serves only to demonstrate the impotence of language in the face of the darkness.

There are similar moments of collapse in Deny's affirmative language when he talks about God as 'Life' for example. Again

[52] Luibheid, 1987, 135: 'Brilliant darkness of a hidden silence ... fill our sightless minds with treasures beyond all beauty.'

his affirmative theology may *look* like a description of God, but it turns out not to be in fact. Denys notes that the Bible talks about God as 'Life':

> Let us now praise Eternal Life, since from it comes life itself and all life, and by it life is appropriately distributed to all who in any way partake of life. From it and through it exist and subsist the life and immortality of the immortal angels, and the indestructibility of the angelic life. ... And the divine Life beyond life is the giver and creator of life itself. All life and living movement comes from a Life which is above every life and is beyond the source of life. From this Life souls have their indestructibility, and every living being and plant, down to the last echo of life, has life.

Again it looks as if Denys knows something about God. He says God is 'Life', *apparently* saying something about him as he is in himself. But as soon as he tries to say what we mean when we talk about God as Life, Denys can't give it any content in relation to God himself. God is the *source* of life in angels, the *source* of life in human beings (their immortal souls) and the *source* of life in lower living beings – even plants. But Denys knows nothing about 'Life' as it applies to God. The only thing he knows are the *effects* of God in living things that he has made. Of course it makes sense to talk of God as 'Life' if he causes all life to exist. But it shouldn't be understood as a description of God. It may be understood as devotional poetry: 'God is Life' might make a good first line of a hymn.

We might say that the expression 'God is Life' is to be understood analogically – and this is perhaps closer to what Denys means. This analogical use of language is important. Let us think of a parallel example. We may call a dog healthy when she's fit, running around, has a cold, wet nose, glossy coat and so on. How, we might ask, did this dog become so healthy?

Well, it is because she has a 'healthy diet'. But when we say 'healthy' about the diet we are not using the word in the same way it was used when we talked about the dog. A healthy diet doesn't run around or have a cold nose. It is 'healthy' because it *causes* health in the dog. Saying the diet is 'healthy' does not tell us what a healthy dog is like. Likewise, calling God 'Life' because he gives life to all living things absolutely does not tell us what God is like.

This is how it goes with Denys's affirmative or cataphatic theology. The pattern is for him to say, 'here is a word which we can use of God, as a name of God'. He talks about God as Being, Light, Truth, Beautiful, Wise, Existent and so on, but immediately applies these words to God's effects rather than God himself. So when he talks of God as Being, he talks not directly about God, but about how he is the cause of being, the things he brings about, or behind which he dwells:

> The God who is transcends everything by virtue of his power. He is the Cause and maker of being, of subsistence, of existence, of substance, and of nature. He is the Source and measure of the ages. He is the reality beneath time and the eternity behind being. ... From Him-who-Is come eternity, essence and being, come time, genesis and becoming. He is the being immanent in and underlying the things which are, however they are. For God is not some kind of being. No, but in a way that is simple and indefinable he gathers into himself and anticipates every existence. So he is called 'King of the Ages', for in him and around him all being is and subsists. He was not. He will not be. He did not come to be. He is not in the midst of becoming. He will not come to be. No. He is not. Rather he is the essence of being for the things which have being.[53]

53   Luibheid, 1987, 98.

So it's fine to speak of God as 'a being', or as 'pure Being', if you want to. But in the end the language collapses again, and Denys says you can only talk of him in this way because of what he brings about as 'the eternity behind being', rather than what he is. What he brings about we can see all around us. But in himself, 'He was not, he will not be ... He is not.' If he is 'the essence of being' for the things which exist, then God cannot be one of those things which exist.

Another feature of Denys' theology is that we can use almost any word, any idea, to describe God. Because all things were made by God, they all bear traces of God in their being, in their beauty, in their truthfulness to their own nature, and so on. Everything in creation has a name, and *all* these names can be used to describe God, precisely because they all bear the traces of God in them.

> Since it [i.e. God] is the Cause of all beings, we should posit and ascribe to it all the affirmations we make in regard to beings, and, more appropriately, we should negate all these affirmations, since it surpasses all beings.[54]

Note that in that passage he says we can use all these names of creatures to speak of the Creator, but adds immediately that we should also 'negate all these affirmations' – again the constant process of affirmation and denial, the collapse of affirmation. Denys is quite unembarrassed about using very earthy images of God.

> I have spoken of the images we have of him, of the forms, figures and instruments proper to him, of the places in which he lives and of the ornaments he wears. I have spoken of his anger, his grief and rage, of how he is said to be drunk and hungover, of his oaths and curses, his

---

[54]   Luibheid, 1987, 136.

sleeping and waking, and indeed of all those images we have of him, images shaped by the workings of the symbolic representations of God.[55]

In some ways it may be better to use these earthier images of God. When you use the higher images, the more pious-sounding ones, the more elevated language like Light, Truth, Beauty, you might be tempted to think that you were beginning to get some kind of a handle on God, that you were getting an idea of what God is actually like. That is why these more elevated images are dangerous. So there are advantages to using the lower and more earthy images, because you are far less likely to make the mistake of thinking you have got information about God when you are talking about him as a rock, or a moth, or a mighty fortress, or even having long nostrils – all of these being biblical images.

But whether you are using the elevated abstract imagery of light and truth, or the homely and earthy imagery of rocks, hangovers and nostrils, none of these gives you information about God himself. They will tell you about the things He has made, all of which come from and return to him, but they will tell us nothing about God.

NOT THIS. NOT THIS.[56]

In *The Divine Names* Denys starts at the highest level of being, with the most elevated of creatures, and shows how all of them have names which can *in some sense* be applied to God, even though none of these names reveals what God is. In his apophatic work – *The Mystical Theology* – he pursues the opposite strategy. He starts at the bottom of creation, among the lowest beings,

[55]   Luibheid, 1987, 139.
[56]   The Sanskrit expression *Neti Neti*, 'not this, not this', expresses in Hindu tradition the equivalent of Denys' method – the constant negation of anything that is.

and denies that God is like any of these. That is straightforward enough: he is clearly not really a rock, or a moth. As he rises up the created order, Denys continues with the process of denial. Here is the grand finale of the *Mystical Theology*:

> Again, as we climb higher we say this. It [God] is not soul or mind, nor does it possess imagination, conviction, speech, or understanding. Nor is it speech per se, understanding per se. It cannot be spoken of and it cannot be grasped by the understanding. It is not number or order, greatness or smallness, equality or inequality, similarity or dissimilarity. It is not immovable, moving or at rest. It has no power, it is not power, nor is it light. It does not live nor is it life. It is not a substance, nor is it eternity or time. It cannot be grasped by the understanding since it is neither knowledge nor truth. It is not kingship. It is not wisdom. It is neither one nor oneness, divinity nor goodness. Nor is it spirit, in the sense in which we understand that term. It is not sonship or fatherhood and it is nothing known to us or to any other being. It falls neither within the predicate of non-being nor of being. Existing beings do not know it as it actually is and it does not know them as they are. There is no speaking of it, nor name nor knowledge of it. Darkness and light, error and truth – it is none of these. It is beyond assertion and denial. We make assertions and denials about what is *next* to it, but never of it, for it is both beyond every assertion, being the perfect and unique cause of all things, and, by virtue of its preeminently simple and absolute nature, free of every limitation, beyond every limitation; it is also beyond every denial.[57]

It is 'the perfect and unique cause of all things'. This is more than simply saying 'God is unknown'. It is saying that too, of

57   Luibheid, 1987, 141.

course, but it is also saying that God is not one of the things which exist, but is rather the reason that anything exists rather than nothing existing at all. It is 'neither non-being nor being ... beyond assertion and denial'.

We might finish our consideration of Denys by looking at a very short letter he wrote in which he addresses 'the monk Gaius'. This addressee may be a literary fiction, inspired by the equally short 'Third Letter of John' in the New Testament which is also addressed to 'the beloved Gaius'. Denys's letter deals with the issue of 'knowing God', and he re-asserts the transcendent darkness of such knowledge: 'He is completely unknown and non-existent. He is beyond being, and is known beyond the mind.'[58] This is now quite familiar language to us, having looked at Denys's other writings. Forget about 'knowing God'. Nothing counts as knowing God except knowing that we don't know. Except perhaps for one thing that Denys hints at by his addressing the letter to 'the monk Gaius', because if this is a reference to the 'beloved Gaius' in the Third Letter of John, then perhaps Denys is leading us a step further. For in John's letter we read, 'He who does good is of God; he who does evil has not seen God.' For John, doing good, loving one another, is what counts as 'seeing God' or 'knowing God'. The whole of Denys's theology points towards 'knowledge of God' as 'knowing nothing', as darkness, but his reference to John's letter suggests that he is pointing towards John's view: there is a way of 'knowing God' or 'seeing God' which is open to us, and it is nothing to do with acquiring information about God, or having an experience of God. It is simply (as we saw in Chapter 4 above) that we love one another.

[58]   Luibheid, 1987, 263.

CHAPTER SEVEN.

THOMAS AQUINAS: ON PROVING NOTHING

IN MANY WAYS Thomas Aquinas is the heart of this book. He is the single most important influence on my way of thinking about God as Nothing. Thomas is where I started from, and then I began looking backwards at other sources (Mesopotamian poetry, Genesis, the Incarnation of Christ) and forwards (to Marx and Feuerbach, Wittgenstein and modern poetry). The idea behind this book really began with my reading of Thomas Aquinas, and commentators on Thomas, and discussions with other people who were interested in Thomas. And perhaps more than anything else, being taught Thomas Aquinas in Oxford in the 1980s by Herbert McCabe – the most gifted of teachers, and a most expert and exciting interpreter of Thomas's writings.

It will perhaps be useful to think a bit about who Thomas was and the time when he was writing – his context. He was born in 1226 into a large aristocratic family in the kingdom of Naples, and in 1231, at the age of five or six, he was sent to study in the Benedictine monastery of Monte Cassino. It seems that his parents hoped that their little son would become a monk and eventually abbot of the monastery with which their family had a long-standing connection. But young Thomas had other ideas. After studying with the Benedictines, he went to the recently-founded university of Naples. Here he was immersed not only in the mainstream traditional sources of Christian thought (Augustine, Jerome, Gregory, Pseudo-Dionysius, John Damascene and so on), but also in new and exciting ideas. The works of Aristotle were just beginning to be translated into Latin, having lain largely unexamined by western thinkers for many centuries. These new ideas were often mediated by Muslim and Jewish scholars, and Thomas recognised the power of their use of Aristotle. He used arguments about the nature of 'being' found in the writings of the Muslim Ibn Sina,[59] and he regularly cited the work of Moses Maimonides, a great Jewish scholar.[60]

In Naples not only did Thomas encounter a lot of new philosophical ideas. He also met a community of Dominican friars, recently founded there in 1231, members of an order which combined a simple monastic life in urban communities with a great enthusiasm for the intellectual life and for preaching, communicating the fruits of their studies to others. In spite of his parents' efforts to get him to be a respectable Benedictine monk, he opted to become a Dominican. The family tried very hard to change his mind, so much so that they kidnapped him and locked him up in the family castle of Roccasecca, trying to dissuade him from his Dominican life by introducing a young woman into a room where he was held captive in the hope that she would seduce him. Finally his mother relented, accepted that he would remain a Dominican, and helped him to escape through a window of the castle while his Dominican brethren were waiting below. They whisked him off to Naples, and he then went to study in Paris, and later in Cologne.

[59]   He uses Ibn Sina (called Avicenna in the west) in one of the 'Five Ways', for example.
[60]   Maimonides died in 1204.

At Cologne, Thomas studied under another Dominican, Albert (now known as 'Albert the Great') who among his vast literary output had written a translation and commentary on Denys's *Mystical Theology*, one of the texts we looked at in the previous chapter. In this work, following Denys, Albert explores the collapse of human language in the face of God; he pursues the insight that God is not to be listed among the things that exist:

> Similarly he [who seeks God] must abandon all that is actually existent and all that is non-existent, being merely potential, because God is not categorized with other things that exist, as if he formed a class with them. And thus he should rise to be united with God, who is above all being and knowledge ... He is to be carried upward to the ray of divine darkness, removing everything.[61]

Thomas himself also worked extensively on Denys and his negative theology, insisting that God is completely 'outside the order of beings'. Denys was one of the most important influences on his thought about this. In many ways, Denys would probably have remained a fairly obscure writer if Albert and Thomas hadn't taken him up with such commitment: the commitment to keeping God out of the world of existing things, commitment to saying that God is beyond knowledge, beyond existence, beyond affirmation and denial.

I think that there is another dimension of Thomas's theology which is sometimes rather underestimated. The fact that he was a Dominican friar meant that he spent his life living in communities which were part of an international order whose foundation, only ten years before he was born, had originally been for a very specific purpose. The Dominicans were initially founded to preach against the Albigensian heresy.

---

[61] Tugwell, 1988, 147-8.

This was a return of the constantly recurring idea that the true and good God had only made souls, spiritual beings, and that some opposing force had made the material world. For the Albigensians, then, the material world was bad, and our bodies were the source of sin and death. Salvation was salvation *from matter*, from bodiliness and so on (we have looked at this idea already). The life of the senses was therefore corrupt because it was part of bodily life, and because the objects of our senses were physical things in the created world. Now as the Dominicans had initially been founded to preach against this heresy, they naturally tended to emphasise the goodness of the created order, the life of the body, food, drink, sexuality and reproduction, the information that our bodily senses acquire from creatures in the world, and so on This also meant that natural reason, thinking rationally about the visible, audible, tangible world which we see, hear and touch, was essential to our human nature. It meant that human knowing is not the speculation of some disembodied mind. All our knowing is rooted in our bodiliness, our animal natures, our physical responses to the world and each other, and the ways of talking that we linguistic animals have invented.

Thomas's teacher, Albert, was a fine exemplar of this tradition of openness to the world. In addition to his more abstract theological and philosophical works – and he wrote a great deal – he was also fascinated by the material world. He wrote works on natural history – the noise made by mating fish, why flies lay their eggs on some walls rather than others. He used to climb up cliffs to count the eggs of nesting birds. He acquired a snake in order to see what happened to it if it got drunk. He carried a lump of iron with him in his pocket, because he had heard that ostriches could eat metal, and he hoped that he might meet an ostrich on his travels and do an experiment to see if it was true. This fascination with the natural and material world was not just incidental to his theology. It was demanded by it. Albert interpreted Psalm 19, 'the heavens proclaim the glory of God', to mean that all creatures sing his praise. And so he said, 'the whole world is theology for us.' Because God's Word or *logos* brought everything into being, the world is *logical* and capable of scientific investigation and explanation. To study the world was understood as an act of confidence and trust in the Creator. And because all creatures proclaim their creator, talking about the world is a way of talking about God; our knowledge of the world is the way we come to know about God. As his student Thomas remarked, 'A mistake about creatures will result in error about God', citing Psalm 28:5, 'Because they do not regard the works of the Lord, or the work of his hands, he will break them down and build them up no more.'[62]

This confidence in our engagement with the world, as we will see, also shaped Thomas's thinking. For Thomas, all knowledge begins with the senses, with what our ears, eyes, noses, picked up.[63] Even what we know about God had to be learned from the life of the senses. Not that we could ever *sense* God, but that we started with the things we knew from our senses, and we struggled from what we knew towards the unknown.

Perhaps that's enough on the background to his writings. But we should bear these details in mind when we are reading Thomas. These are the assumptions that shaped all his writing – his commentaries on Aristotle, his Bible commentaries, his theological writings, his language, and of course his life.

MYSTICISM AND CLARITY

Thomas is sometimes thought of as an immensely logical writer, with clear arguments using precisely defined terms, and therefore someone who is not particularly mystical. This is because the popular idea of mysticism is that it is a

---

[62] Aquinas, *Summa Contra Gentiles*, 2, 3. The section is headed, 'Knowledge of creatures is able to break down errors about God.'

[63] For example *Summa Theologiae* 1a, 84, 6.

rather touchy-feely sort of thing. It is often thought to be all about inner experience, a slightly warm and fuzzy feeling of closeness. But in Thomas's view, God *can't* be an object of experience. We may have all kinds of experiences, and some of them we may describe as religious experiences in some way, but none of them are experiences of God as the *object* of experience. We may have experiences of a relationship, a song, a death, the way low winter light strikes a tree, or a sudden thought – those are objects of experience. We may be profoundly inspired by a poem, a mathematical formula, a sermon, or a reading from some sacred text which we hear just at that moment when it is exactly what we need to hear. But among all these, God is not the object of the experience. For Thomas, God cannot literally be an object of experience, because God is not one of the 'objects available' for experience. You can't ask except in a joke (or as part of a philosophical enquiry, which may be the same kind of thing), 'Was that an experience of God, or an experience of my mother-in-law?' These are not two alternative objects of experience, because they are not two alternative beings. In another sense, of course, an experience of your mother-in-law could be 'an experience of God' (though God would not be the object of experience), but that is also because God and your mother-in-law are not two alternative beings. God cannot be listed among the things which are potential objects of experience, because God cannot be included on any list. This is what Thomas means when he insists (as he does repeatedly) that God is not a member of any *genus*, any category or kind.[64] So if you make a list of any kind of thing (persons, causes, objects of experience, etc.), if 'God' is on that list you have misunderstood the way the word 'God' is properly used in Christian theology.

As I have just suggested, however, you may want to say that you feel or intuit a depth of meaning in some experience

---

[64] *Summa Theologiae*, 1a, 3, art. 5. for example.

(solitude, having children, prayer, friendship, the phenomenal processes of evolution), and you may want to call this depth of meaning an 'experience of God' or something like that. It may be that this experience makes you feel loved, forgiven, strengthened, inspired – the kind of things that people say God does to them – but that does not make God the *object* of our experience. It means that our experience of 'something' has helped us to understand or intuit something about our union with God.

Now I want to say that Thomas, for all his rationality, for all the clarity and precision of his language and his careful sifting of arguments, is a true mystic. He is a mystic not because he was overwhelmed by certain feelings (though he was in fact overwhelmed in various ways). He is a mystic in the sense that he is always aware of the complete mystery of the Unknown God – 'to know God,' he writes, 'is to know that we don't know what he is'. But at the same time he is aware that we ourselves are intimately united to this God – 'we are joined to him as to the unknown'.[65] Mysticism is not about fuzziness or romantic language and purple prose. It's about the union of the person with the terrifying mystery of God, and there is no better way of making the mystery of God clear than by painstaking intellectual rigour, gradually demolishing all the images and idols that seduce us, sweeping away the gods, confronting us with the darkness of our unknowing.

THE FIVE WAYS

To illustrate this we may look at one of the passages in Thomas's writings. It is from his *Summa Theologiae*, a great work that he wrote in the last decade or so of his life. When I say 'great', I partly mean 'big'; in the bilingual edition (Latin and English) it occupies 60 volumes. It is his best known and most referenced work, and perhaps that is because of the

---

[65] *Summa Theologiae* 1a, 12, xiii ad primum: 'ei quasi ignoto coniungamur'.

clarity of the writing. It is also much less dense and technical than some of his work, and he explains each step of his argument as he goes along very clearly, because it was written not for professional theologians, but for the young Dominican students that Thomas was teaching, friars who would not all be intellectuals in the universities, but preachers in the towns all over Europe. Thomas thought that you should still have a sound theological education, even if you weren't destined to become a professional theologian.

There is a broad all-embracing architecture to the *Summa*. It begins with God himself, his 'existence', how we may (or may not) talk about him, what it means to talk about his 'knowledge', his 'will', the Trinity, eternity and so on. And from God himself the *Summa* follows the 'downward' sweep of Creation, how all that exists is made and ordered by God, the creation and nature of humanity, the happiness that we are created for, human morality and the sin which has undone us. The turning point in this architecture, the 'keystone' of the arch if you like, is the Gospel of Christ, the crucified and risen one.[66] The rest of the work (which is actually incomplete) follows the way that the fallen human race is drawn back to God by Christ, by faith, hope and love. The virtues (prudence, temperance, courage, justice and others) are restored in us; the sacraments are celebrated in the shadow of the cross and restore us to ourselves. But they do more than restore our fallen humanity; they also bring us to share in the life of God, becoming divine ourselves.

So much for the great sweep of the *Summa*. The passage we will look at is from the earliest part of the work, the second question. Now it *seems* to be (and indeed it is often called) a series of five 'proofs of the existence of God'. This second question of the *Summa* is divided into three short 'articles'.

---

[66] Thomas speaks of Christ and his salvation at this key point as 'the consummation of the whole theological business' (*consummationem totius theologici negotii*) (*Summa Theologiae*, 3a, prologue).

The first article asks whether the existence of God is self-evident. Does the very idea of God guarantee the existence of God? There were theologians who thought it did – Anselm for example – but Thomas denies it. He also refers to John Damascene who says that knowledge of the existence of God is naturally implanted in everyone, but Thomas denies that too.[67] You are going to have to use your brain to think about this, he implies. You will have to argue about it. After all, Thomas points out, the Bible itself points to people who deny the existence of God, so clearly God's existence cannot be self-evident.

But although Thomas thought that God's existence was not philosophically self-evident, we should bear in mind that he lived in a world where by and large people simply assumed the existence of God. There was little of what we might now recognise as philosophical atheism in western Europe in the thirteenth century. People weren't muttering darkly in the taverns around the new universities, 'Perhaps there is no God after all.'[68] So when we turn to the second and third articles of this question in the *Summa*, we might ask what exactly Thomas was trying to do. People often treat these articles as ways of 'proving the existence of God', attempting to refute the view of a speculative philosophical atheist. But if Thomas has never come across a speculative atheist, why would he want to 'prove the existence of God'? Who is he proving it to? As we read these 'proofs' we should perhaps consider that he is doing something rather different from refuting atheism. Maybe he is demonstrating something else. We'll think a bit more about this shortly.

Article one showed that God's existence was not self-

---

[67] *Summa Theologiae* 1a, 2, art. 1, ad primum.

[68] This cannot have been because people were too frightened to express an atheistic viewpoint. There was an enormous amount of dissent about all kinds of things, and we know about all kinds of dissident ideas which were regarded by church authorities as heretical. But atheism wasn't generally part of the repertoire of dissent.

evident. Article two now seeks to show that, even if it is not *self-evident*, it can at least be *argued* for. He says God's *esse*, God's being or 'to be' (the infinitive form of the verb), is demonstrable. He says that any effect must have a cause, and as the effect depends on the cause, so the cause must have pre-existed the effect. We cannot approach God directly to study him, but we can nevertheless learn to talk about God by studying his effects in his creatures. He quotes St Paul: 'The invisible nature of God is perceived through our understanding of the things that have been made' (Romans 1:20). We can learn to think about the cause by studying the effects. The existence of created things demonstrates something of the creator: 'by effects we proceed to knowledge of the cause'. Thus, he says, though God is not known or demonstrable *per se*, his being or *esse* can be inferred from his effects.

You might not find this entirely convincing. Of course, effects have causes. But to describe the whole world as an 'effect' is already to assume that it has a cause. The atheist doesn't say that the world is an effect without a cause; she says that it isn't an effect at all, and so the question of there being a cause doesn't arise.[69] But at this point Thomas is not arguing against atheism; he is arguing against people who say that the real world of things can tell us nothing about God, who think the creatures that we see and touch, the things we eat and bump into every day, with their materiality and their smell, their provisionalness, are irrelevant to our faith in God. Thomas is insisting that this real creaturely world is the only reason we can talk about God at all. All this sensed reality is revelation: even if it tells us nothing of what God is like (we cannot know), nor about what it might mean to say that 'God

---

[69] Thomas might very well respond to this: When we see that something is the case when it might not have been the case, we may ask 'Why?' The existence of the world is the case, and it might not have been the case. So there is no good reason to refuse to ask the question 'Why does the world exist, rather than nothing?'.

exists', it still enables us to speak in some way about God.

Finally in the third article of this question – the article most often treated as 'proofs of the existence of God' – Thomas asks simply *utrum Deus sit*. This is usually translated as 'whether God exists'. That's a perfectly reasonable translation, but notice that it has the same grammatical form as 'whether unicorns exist'. Now, in order to answer the question whether unicorns exist we would first have to know what a unicorn was and then look around to see if we could find one, or find any evidence of such a thing existing (grainy footage from a camera trap, hoof-prints of a particular sort, horn-marks on the bark of a tree or such like). But we can only start looking for it, or for evidence of it, once we have decided what a unicorn is. But Thomas says quite unequivocally that in the case of God we don't know what he is; therefore we don't know what we are looking for. So to ask the question 'whether God exists' in the way we asked it about unicorns would be simply impossible. This puts a slightly different 'spin' on the question. It might mean simply looking at everything which exists and asking, 'Is it meaningful to talk about "God" given all this existing stuff?' As you can see, it doesn't require us to say what God is at all; it invites us rather to look at all that exists in a particular way, seeing it as dependent, as explicable, perhaps even as a gift. We might translate *utrum Deus sit* as 'whether there is God'. And the word 'God' here is simply the word we use to express this way of seeing what exists. It is not the name of some 'individual being' that we can look for.

It is to answer this question, 'whether there is God', that Thomas offers his famous 'Five Ways', five short arguments. They are generally called 'proofs of the existence of God', and it is not surprising given the way that he introduces them. He writes, *Respondeo dicendum quod Deum esse quinque viis probari potest*, which might be translated, 'I reply that God may be proved to be in five ways'. That is perhaps the most obvious way of translating the sentence, but maybe it is not quite right.

For one thing, as we have seen, to prove the existence of X we have to know what X is, whether it is a unicorn or God; and we have no idea what God is, only what he is not, according to Thomas himself.[70] But secondly, what is the weight of *probari* in this sentence? It is the passive form of the verb *probare*, which is usually translated 'to prove', and in modern English that generally implies an argument of evidence and reason which leads inevitably to a certain conclusion. I can 'prove' that the three angles of a triangle add up to 180 degrees (or I used to be able to when I was at school). But Latin *probare* has a range of meanings: 'to represent as good, to make acceptable, to make credible', for example. And there are other meanings which may be closer to what Thomas intends: it means 'to test' or 'to inspect'. These are meanings that do not imply the establishment of a 'fact' by irresistible logic, but a rather more tentative process. A bit like 'the proof of the pudding is in the eating', it's about trying something out, testing it – in this case testing the idea that 'there is God' and what on earth we might mean when we say such a thing. Indeed, the Latin word *probare* is the origin of English 'probe', which means exactly this kind of trying and testing.

So let us look at one of these so-called Five Ways. The first of them is an argument based on *motus* which means 'motion' or 'change', and it proceeds like this:

> The first and clearest way (*via*) is from the understanding of change (*motus*).[71] For it is sure, and our senses confirm, that things in this world undergo change. Everything

---

[70]   *De Deo scire non possumus quid sit, sed quid non sit*, 'Concerning God, we can not know what he is, but only what he is not' (*Summa Theologiae* Ia.3, prologue).

[71]   This is usually translated 'movement', and God as the 'unmoved mover', but 'movement' in English usually just means physical change of an object in space, while Thomas implies a broader sense of *any* change – a change in temperature for example, which in colloquial English would not normally be described as 'movement'.

which changes is changed by something else. Nothing changes unless it has the potential to be changed into what it changes into. However, what brings about that change must be something that is already in act [i.e. something actual rather than merely potential]. To change something is simply to lead it from its potency to its actuality. A thing can only be led from a potential to an actuality by something else that is in act. .... Everything therefore which changes must be changed by something else. If therefore the thing by which it is changed itself changes, it must be that that thing is also changed by something else, and that in turn by something else. This process, however, cannot be extended to infinity; for this would mean that there was no first changer. And if that were the case there wouldn't be any other changing thing either, for all subsequent changing things would not change unless by the things that were changed by the first changer, just as a stick cannot move except by the thing that is moved by the hand. Therefore we must necessarily come to the First Changer, which is not changed by anything, and everyone understands this as 'God'.

There are all kinds of weaknesses with this argument if we read it simply as an attempt to establish logically that 'God *must* exist'. Thomas could be challenged, for example, on his statement that this process of causing change 'cannot be extended to infinity'. It is not at all obvious that this is so. In fact, Thomas himself taught that it was perfectly possible for God to have made an infinite world, and it is only the Bible that tells him that the universe had a beginning.[72] However, even if there were an infinite series of change-causing actors, one could still treat that whole infinite universe of changes

---

[72]   He writes about this at length in *De aeternitate mundi contra murmu-rantes*, explaining that there are no philosophical objections to the world having always existed, but only the teaching of *scriptura sacra*, the Bible.

as itself being an instance of change and ask, 'Why is all this change going on, rather than no change at all?' The answer to this question, 'Why is there any change rather than none?' cannot be something which itself changes. This may not prove the existence of God in the sense of a logical demonstration that he exists. But it does 'probe' or 'test' the existence of God – that other sense of *probare* – and it leads us towards an idea: whatever we mean by 'God' it must be utterly beyond the world of change.

Then we may consider Thomas's second 'Way' in which he considers the world as the place where things cause other things.

> The second way follows the logic of efficient causes. For we find among sensible objects that there is an order of efficient causes. And nothing is to be found, nor is it possible, that is its own efficient cause, for such a thing would have to be prior to itself, which is impossible. Now in efficient causes there cannot be an infinite regress. For in all efficient causes, the first is the cause of the middle, the middle is the cause of the last (the middle cause may be multiple or singular). If you take away the cause, you take away the effect. Therefore, if there were not a first of all efficient causes, there would not be an ultimate effect, nor any intermediate cause. But if you were to proceed to infinity with efficient causes, then there would not be a first efficient cause. And in that case there would be no ultimate effect, nor any intermediate efficient causes, and that is patently false. Therefore it is necessary to propose some first efficient cause, and this everyone calls 'God'.

Once again, we may disagree with Thomas on the impossibility of 'an infinite regress'. Some people may be quite happy to think of a regress of causes going back over an infinite period of time, without beginning or end. But Thomas will then ask, why does this infinite regress of causation exist at all when it might not have existed? What caused this infinite regress? Here we are not thinking of the first cause in a long line of causes, but rather the overall cause of all the causes and all the effects – the whole universe of cause and effect.

When Thomas talks of such efficient causes he is discussing the world of the natural sciences, where we try to understand how some things in the world cause other things to happen. We are in the world of scientific causality, a world where we can identify certain 'rules' in the way some things in the world cause other things. That's what scientists do, so that once they understand why things behave in a certain way, they can predict things that will happen under certain circumstances. The fact that causation takes place in the world in a more or less regular way makes scientific explanation possible. The question arises then, 'Why is there a universe in which scientific explanation is possible?' The answer to this question, which Thomas says everyone calls 'God', *cannot* be something which is part of the world of scientific explanations. God's creating of this world, therefore, cannot be a scientific explanation of. anything. So God cannot be a 'cause' in the sense that the interactions within the world are causes, for if he were he would be part of that world of causes which we are trying to explain.

Once again, we may or may not think that this argument works as a proof or logical demonstration of the existence of something called 'God', but it is better seen as a way of 'probing' or 'testing' what we mean when we say, 'there is God'. And whatever we mean, it *cannot* be part of the world of causes, not even the first one of a long line of causes. It is the reason a world of causes exists at all, rather than nothing existing.

We should remember the question that was raised earlier: if this was a logical proof or demonstration of the existence of God, who was he proving it *to*? He is a thirteenth-century European, surrounded by people who take the presence of God for granted. And we should also remember what we said earlier about proving the existence of something: to prove the existence of X you need to know what X is. But that is precisely what Thomas denies with regard to God. We don't know what he is. Indeed, it is surely no coincidence that immediately after these 'Five Ways' Thomas goes on immediately to state precisely the opposite:

> Once you know that something exists, it remains to enquire how it is, so that you may know what it is. But since we cannot know what God is, we cannot consider how God is, either, but rather how he is not. So we must first consider how he is not, and secondly how we can know him, and thirdly how we can speak of him.

Thomas says this over and over again. We do not know, nor can we ever know in this life, what God is, what his nature is. We can say all kinds of things about God – by negation (i.e. by denying all kinds of things about him), by metaphor, by analogy, and by saying things about his effects, his creatures. But none of these things tells us what God is.

Since Thomas cannot be in any obvious sense 'proving that God exists', because he can't define what God is, we should perhaps be reading him as probing and testing our ideas about God, our too-easy assumptions about how we use the word, what we think God is. He is inviting us to share in the 'brilliant darkness' of his own mystical vision. If we are seduced by the language we use into thinking it has given us a 'handle' on God, information about him, Thomas brings us up short. When we speak of God, we draw mental pictures of a being who exists alongside us which we call 'God', but Thomas, faithful to the tradition of Pseudo-Dionysius, shows that even if we do draw such pictures we must continually erase them.

Note that none of the proofs say anything about God in himself at all. They all speak about the world. The two we looked at simply examine the world and see that it is full of change, and full of things which cause other things. These observed facts raise the radical question of why such a world exists at all. Thomas simply infers from the facts of the world that there is a mystery. The very existence of the world, and the fact it is provisional, changeable, full of cause and effect, and so on, raises a fundamental question, points to a mystery, and he says of this mystery: *quam omnes Deum nominant*, 'everyone calls it God.'

It remains always a mystery. The point of these so-called proofs is to lend support to his doctrine of unknowing, not to undermine it. The point of the proofs is to point towards the mystery which surrounds the world, which is the mystery of existence: why is there anything rather than nothing? It is not to define the mystery, but rather to test the way we use the word 'God', and to establish ways of talking which will *prevent* us from claiming to know things about God. His 'proofs' point to an unknown which is radically *other*, which is outside the world of things, and therefore not a 'something' at all.

For Thomas, we will know what God is only in death, when we have been taken beyond the world of language and thinking, when God will make us gods. Human beings were not destined to become merely improved, or even perfect, men and women, but to share in the divine life, and thus to share in God's self-knowledge.[73] This is 'knowledge' beyond thought or image or language. At the end of his life Thomas seems to have had some kind of vision during the celebration of the Mass one

---

[73]   This touches on the idea, which Thomas inherited from Augustine, that because of our being made in the image of God, the human mind is *capax Dei*, 'has a capacity for God'. That is to say we are created by nature with all kinds of capacities, almost all of which can be satisfied by other finite created goods. But one of our capacities – the most important of all - is a capacity for God which is infinite and cannot be satisfied by anything other than God himself. See *Quaestiones disputatae, De veritate*, q. 22, art. 2 and *ad quintum*: 'Only a rational creature has the capacity for God (*est capax Dei*), for only it can know and love him explicitly. But other creatures also share in the divine likeness, and so tend towards him.'

day in 1273. He returned to his work – he was still working on the *Summa Theologiae* at the time – but wrote nothing. His brothers were worried that he was depressed or ill. His friend Reginald, urged him to start writing again, to finish the *Summa*, but Thomas replied, 'Everything I have written seems like straw in comparison to what I have seen and what has been revealed to me.'

This was not a new discovery for Thomas, though. When he said his writings were straw, implying that no matter how clear and methodical and precise his huge corpus of work was, it would still not be able to show us what God was like, this was nothing new. He had been asserting this from the very beginning. He had said again and again that God was beyond speech – but that was why he kept talking and writing, and why he kept talking and writing with such fierce clarity and precision. It's easy to talk about God in vague and fuzzy ways, and if those ways of talking break down under close inspection, then no one is very surprised. You expect vague ways of talking to break down at some point. But Thomas wants to show that even the most careful and rational language, the most painstaking precision, also breaks down. In this life, all language breaks down in the presence of God, in the darkness of unknowing.[74] All that clarity and precision were always intended precisely for this: to show that God was not any kind of thing, that there was no God in the universe, and that whatever we meant by the word 'God' it must be *omnino extra ordinem entium*,[75] 'completely outside the order of beings'.

---

[74] Josef Pieper puts this notion very well: 'He who fears the bold light of logic will never penetrate into the region of real mysteries. The man who does not use his reason will never get to that boundary beyond which reason really fails. In the work of St Thomas all ways of creaturely knowing have been followed to the very end – to the boundary of mystery. And the more intensely we pursue these ways of knowledge, the more is revealed to us of the *darkness*, but also of the *reality* of mystery' (1957, 44).

[75] Thomas Aquinas, *In Peri Hermeneias*, I, xiv (p. 73).

FINDING OUR WAY

We might say that Thomas's mysticism leaves us with a few pointers. We are travellers through a bewildering landscape, moving towards a destination we don't know, but to which we are drawn by desire. In this landscape, perhaps some of Thomas's pointers can be imagined as landmarks which help us to orientate ourselves.

- God, as the Creator of all that exists, cannot be one of the things which exist. He is 'completely outside the order of beings'.
- God is not a member of any class of things – *non est in genere.*
- As the Creator, God cannot occupy any space or time – since space and time are features of Creation.
- If God does not occupy any time, there can be no 'before' or 'after', but is eternal (completely outside time or succession).
- If God does not have a 'before' or 'after', he must be beyond all change, because a change is always from one state to another, before and after states.
- If God is the Creator, then *everything* comes from him.
- He doesn't set things up and 'allow' things to happen. All that exists, and everything that it does, is simply and immediately the effect of his creative act.
- If God is the Creator of every being and every event in the world, nothing can 'happen to' God.
- Speaking of of God's 'knowledge', Thomas says it is very different from ours. God's knowledge is the *cause* of things existing, whereas existing things are the cause of our knowledge of them as they imprint themselves on our minds.
- Likewise, God does not love things because they are good. They are good because he loves them. We, on the other hand, love them *because* they are good. Their goodness is what causes our love.

Some of these points appear in various guises elsewhere in this book, especially in the *Refractions* section at the end. But it seems useful to list them here in their starkest and simplest forms, since it is in Thomas's writing that they achieve their clearest, starkest and sometimes shocking form.

CHAPTER EIGHT.

ECKHART: BECOMING NOTHING, BECOMING GOD

SO FAR, WE have been looking at writings which are fairly central to the Christian tradition. In this chapter, however, we are going to be looking at someone who is rather more marginal. A lot of Christians have never heard of him, though he did in fact exercise some influence over late medieval thought and practice. Eckhart was born around the year 1260, near Erfurt in Thuringia. There is almost nothing known about his family background. He appears on the historical horizon at the age of about 15, when he first enters the Dominican order as a novice.

As soon as we learn that Eckhart was a Dominican we must think of Thomas Aquinas, another Dominican whom we discussed in the previous chapter, and his Dominican teacher in Cologne, Albert the Great. Eckhart is part of this same school of thought, and part of the same religious movement in medieval Europe. Indeed he may even have been taught by Albert in Cologne – he will certainly have met him, since in the summer of 1280 Eckhart was in the Dominican friary in Cologne, and Albert died in that house later that year. If Eckhart wasn't taught by Albert himself, he will surely have been taught by some of Albert's colleagues there. So he was drinking from the same intellectual and spiritual well as those scholars who had been taught by Albert and Thomas.[76] He came under the influence, just as they had, of Pseudo-Dionysius and that radically negative or apophatic theology. Another important influence on Eckhart, interestingly, was the writing of Muslim and Jewish theologians, especially Moses Maimonides (Eckhart always calls him, with deep respect, Rabbi Moses).

After studying at Cologne, Eckhart was sent to Paris as a lecturer, and there he obtained the title of Master of Theology – the highest title accorded to a theologian in the medieval schools. It's interesting that he is the only one who is still given that title now, when people talk of him: Meister Eckhart.

Eckhart, like most Dominican friars, spent his life juggling different kinds of jobs. In addition to scholarly work he was given various positions of authority within the order, clearly enjoying the confidence of his brethren. And of course he was a priest and a preacher, a guide to various groups of nuns and other religious groups during a period of a great revival of 'spiritual life' and lay activity – enthusiastic communities of men and women trying to find more serious, more committed, more intellectually rigorous ways of living the Gospel.

A good deal of Eckhart's writing has survived and is available in modern English translation.[77] His academic writings were mostly in Latin, dense, complex, hard to understand. His devotional writings – mostly sermons – were written in Middle High German. Indeed, Eckhart's vernacular

[76] Thomas Aquinas had already died in 1274, so Eckhart is unlikely to have met him. But he was surely immersed in Thomas' teaching and ideas, his theological method and views, which were becoming enormously important in Dominican communities and universities where his works were widely circulated.

[77] Walshe 1979; Colledge and McGinn, 1981; McGinn, 1986 (see Bibliography for details). See also the insightful discussion of Eckhart's writing in Denys Turner, *The Darkness of God* (Cambridge, 1995).

writings are some of the best German literature of the period – even apart from their theological interest. It is dramatic and earthy writing. It uses some of the erotic language of desire that had appeared a century earlier in German courtly love poetry.[78] He uses this language to shock his hearers, to destabilise their understanding, to break down the concepts by which they normally and comfortably think about God. That's all very well, but it doesn't make for tidy theology, and sometimes it left him open to being misunderstood. Sometimes he appears to contradict himself, though perhaps this contradiction is more apparent than real, and is really rather a way of thinking using paradox. Perhaps sometimes he got carried away by the energy of his own rhetoric. Some of his contemporaries suspected him of heresy, and in 1325 two Dominicans in Cologne denounced him to the Archbishop of that city. He denied all the charges of heresy, claiming that his accusers were motivated by malice and jealousy. Nevertheless he was found guilty. He appealed to the Pope, with the support of his Dominican superiors and fellow Dominicans, and at the age of about 67 he walked from Cologne to the papal court at Avignon – a distance of about 500 miles – to defend himself.

He was vigorous in defending his views. Those who accused him of heresy, he said (and there may be much truth in this) had not read his works, or if they had read them, they had not understood them. He died in 1327 before his appeal had been fully heard, while it was still going on. Two years later, the pope issued a Bull of Condemnation (*In Agro Dominico*) listing a number of teachings which it condemned as either actually erroneous or potentially misleading. There was some doubt, however, about the extent to which these doctrines were actually taught by Eckhart. In some cases the doctrines condemned were things that he himself had condemned. In

---

[78] McGinn notes that this love poetry (*Minnesang*) had itself originally borrowed much of its energy from the earlier religious poetry exploring the love of God and man (1986, xiii).

other cases, it seems as though the people responsible for investigating his works had not really understood them, as he had protested. His German writings especially need to be read in context, and they need to be read as the kind of rhetorical utterance they are, as poetically suggestive, as deliberately paradoxical and provocative, rather than carefully constructed analytical writing.

Another important point to bear in mind is that Eckhart was writing at a time when there were other movements which were condemned as heretical, and some of their teaching did bear a resemblance to his. In particular there was a movement called 'The Brethren of the Free Spirit'. These people held that in this life it was possible to acquire such perfect union with God that you could move completely beyond the ordinary conditions of human existence. As a Free Spirit you could do away with prayer and devotion of any sort. You could also do away with morality. In 1367 the Free Spirit Johann Hartmann testified that all private property was wrong, and that work (which produced private property) was a sin against nature. 'But a free man, he said – (a Free Spirit, such as himself) – is lord of all creatures. All things belong to him, and he has the right to use whatever pleases him. If someone tries to prevent him, the free man may kill him and take his goods.' His freedom also allowed him to have sex with any woman, anywhere, even with his mother or daughter (is this a peculiarly male fantasy of freedom?). If he had sex with a virgin, she would not lose her virginity. If he had sex with a woman who was not a virgin, she would become a virgin again. The freedom of the Brethren made them free from all secular and religious authority – no law had any hold on them, except the individual will of each one of them, and that individual will was *ipso facto* God's will once you had received the Free Spirit, because God was dwelling in you. For the Free Spirit, 'Whatever your eye sees and desires, let your hand grasp it.'

An unsympathetic reader of Eckhart might suggest that

he shared this view, but a careful reading of his works, placing 'suspect' passages in context, makes it quite clear that he taught precisely the opposite. He was deeply opposed to any kind of selfishness, any kind of possessiveness; for him the whole of Christian life was about loss of self, dispossession. And in fact, in some passages he seems to be arguing precisely *against* those Free Spirit attitudes (though he doesn't actually name them):

> Now some people say, 'If I possess God and God's love, I can do anything I want.' They do not understand these words correctly. As long as you can do anything against God and his commandments, you do not have the love of God, although you may fool the world into thinking that you have it. The person who is established in God's will and God's love finds it delightful to do all the things that are pleasing to God and to avoid doing those that are against God.[79]

This view clearly differentiates Eckhart from those who asserted the right to 'use whatever they please'.

TALKING ABOUT GOD

But our interest here is not in Eckhart's ethics, nor particularly in his defence against accusations of heresy, but in how the idea of 'God as Nothing' may be present in his writings. In the tradition of Pseudo-Dionysius and Thomas Aquinas, sharing their sense of the impossibility of knowing (or uttering) what God is, he explores the ways we can use God-language, always with a sense that the mystery of God is beyond what we can say. He recognises that we stand on the ground of language, and that language engenders images. God speaks to us using images, and we must speak of God using images, but these images do not reveal what God is. They speak of his effects,

---

[79] McGinn 1986, 288.

of the things that exist in the world from God's creative act. They speak of things that we understand, however imperfectly (justice, mercy, anger, power), but Eckhart is unequivocal about the limits of such language: they tell us of the effects of God's creative love, but not about God himself. And above all, for Eckhart, these terms speak of things which are 'many', which are multi-faceted, which are distinct from each other, while God is absolute unity; he is One. Like Thomas therefore, Eckhart observes that negative statements about God are more true than positive statements. Citing Rabbi Moses Maimonides with approval he says:

> He says, 'Know that a negative proposition about the Creator is true; there is nothing doubtful in it nor does it detract from the Creator's truth in any way. But an affirmative proposition about him is partly equivocal.'[80]

Negations are the truest thing we can say about God, because he is beyond all affirmation. Affirmative propositions may mislead us into thinking that they have told us what God is like, whereas God remains always unknown. Likewise Eckhart says, 'all things that are positively said about God, even if they are perfections in us ('just', 'good', 'beautiful'), they are no longer so in God, and they are not more perfect than their opposites.'

Eckhart follows Thomas Aquinas in giving a special significance to the self-disclosure of God in Exodus 3:14. When Moses asks who he should say has sent him to the people of Israel, God replies, 'I am who I am' ('ehyeh asher 'ehyeh). For Thomas this reveals God as pure being. Not 'a being', who could

---

[80] McGinn 1986, 54. Elsewhere he writes: 'Whatever you add by way of negative names with regard to the Creator, you come nearer to grasping him and will come closer to him than the person who does not know how to *remove* from God the perfections and attributes that have been proven to be far from him. ... Rabbi Moses says, "Our understanding in his case is a distancing rather than approach to grasping him."' (McGinn 1986, 101).

be numbered among other beings, but being itself, pure *esse*, pure being. All existing creatures *have* being, as well as their essences; their essence and their being are distinct. But there is no such distinction in God, for the essence of God is being itself. For Thomas therefore God's name *Qui est*, '[He] who is', is more appropriate to God than the word 'God', because of the unrestricted way in which it signifies him.[81] This Latin *qui est* comes from the four-letter Hebrew form of God's name YHWH (which Thomas and Eckhart call *Tetragrammaton*). Eckhart wants to say that of all the things we say about God it is this *esse* or 'to be' itself that is most proper, or the least improper.

Eckhart also lays great stress on the One-ness of God. But this is not numerical one-ness. It is not that 'there is only one' such being, as opposed to many.[82] That would be what Eckhart thinks of as numerical one-ness, and it would require us to 'count God', and so to know something about God, which is impossible. There is not 'one God' in the sense that I am 'one person'. I can be one person, as he says, by denying that I am some other creature. I can be distinguished. I am one because I am finite, I have edges, boundaries, and beyond my boundaries are other distinct creatures. My oneness is numerical, and it depends on me occupying a world in which various discrete entities co-exist and can be distinguished from each other and counted. But God does not live in any world. He does not occupy any space; he is not alongside anything else. The one-ness of God is for Eckhart simply the negation of any multiplicity. God is infinite, and all that exists exists *in him*. Just as the fact that God is pure being or *esse* means he is not 'a being', so his being One means he is beyond all numbering, all differentiation, all distinction, all individuation.

---

[81] *Summa Theologiae* 1a, 13, 12.

[82] 'The unity which makes God One is not the unity that creates number or the principle that constitutes number. Hence as often as you repeat that unity, it would never make a number or make something to be numbered.' (McGinn 1986, 63).

> Creatures, by the fact that they are from the One and below the One, necessarily fall into number, plurality, distinction .... a condition by which they are numbered among the things that are. ... Everything that exists is either above all and above number, or it is numbered among all things. But above all and outside number there is only the One. No difference at all is or can be in the One. ... Rabbi Moses says that God is one 'in all ways and according to every respect,' so that any 'multiplicity either in intellect or in reality is not found in him.' Anyone who beholds 'two' or beholds distinction does not behold God, for God is One, outside and beyond number, and is not counted with anything.[83]

That is to say, the one-ness of God does not make him an individual being. You can't say God is 'one', and I am 'one', and therefore we are two. 'Anyone who beholds two (say, God and myself) does not behold God'. God is not 'one of anything'. He is simply One. Just as he is not 'a being', but simply Being.

GOD AS NOTHING, AS BEING

There are many moments in Eckhart's writing where he argues that God is not the name of any being or individual - that God is not any thing. Sometimes he addresses the question head-on, at other times he passes over it without too much comment, but the idea is the constant underpinning of his thought.

> People imagine that they have more if they have things *and* God than if they have only God but not things. But this is wrong, because all things taken together with God are not more than God alone, by himself.[84]

If God were one of the things that existed, then God plus other things would be more than God alone. But that is not the case.

[83]   McGinn 1986, 32.
[84]   McGinn 1986, 293-4.

All things exist *in* God, created and held in being by God who is the *esse* which grounds their being. God-and-things cannot therefore be added together.

Another passage where Eckhart articulates his idea of God as Nothing with some conviction is in his reading of a passage in the Acts of the Apostles where Saul, intent on persecuting the followers of Christ, is overcome by a brilliant light.[85] The voice of Christ asks him, 'Saul, Saul, why do you persecute me?' After this extreme encounter we are told, 'Saul rose from the ground, and when his eyes were opened, he could see nothing.' Here is Eckhart's interpretation of the story:

> 'Saul got up from the ground, and when he opened his eyes he saw nothing.' It seems to me that this little word, 'nothing', has four meanings. One meaning is: When he got up from the ground with eyes open, he saw nothing, and the nothing was God; for when he saw God, Luke [the supposed author of Acts] calls it a 'nothing'. The second meaning: When he got up, he saw nothing *but* God. The third meaning: in all things he saw nothing but God. The fourth meaning: when he saw God, he viewed all things as nothing.[86]
>
> … Paul rose from the ground and with eyes open he saw nothing. I cannot see what is One. He saw the nothing which was God. God is a nothing and he is a something. Whatever [creature] is something is also nothing. Whatever God is, he is completely. The illumined Dionysius speaks of this when he writes of God: 'He is above being, he is above life, he is above light.' He does not attribute this or that to him and he thinks that he is an I-know-not-what that is utterly above this or that. Whoever sees anything or if anything comes to your attention, it is not God, because

---

85 Acts 9.
86 McGinn 1986, 320.

he is neither this nor that. ... The light that is God shines in the darkness. God is a true light. Whoever is to see this must be blind and must completely remove all 'something' from God. A master says, 'Whoever speaks of God through a simile speaks of him in an impure fashion. But whoever speaks of God by *nothing* speaks of him properly.' When the [human] soul comes into the One and enters into a pure rejection of itself, it finds God as in a nothing. [87]

The encounter with God, 'seeing God', is experienced as a blinding light which makes Saul see *nothing*, and it is precisely in seeing nothing that He 'sees God'.

BECOMING NOTHING, BECOMING GOD

So far, in spite of the dramatic imagery which Eckhart uses, his apophatic theology will be fairly familiar to anyone who has read Pseudo-Dionysius or Thomas Aquinas, or other teachers in that tradition. But Eckhart goes further than this, because he wants to relate the 'nothingness of God' to our own nothingness, and our own voyage *into* God. Just as God lies beyond all something-ness, beyond any attribute we might imagine, in the silence of eternity, and to speak of him we must strip him of all language, all images, so Eckhart also speaks of the human soul. To find God in ourselves (or rather to find ourselves in God, as opposed to merely speaking of him) we must also strip ourselves. This is because we are made in the image of God. Just as there is Nothing at the heart of God's being, we must seek to make ourselves nothing to share in that divine life.

Underlying this is Eckhart's view that there is a likeness between the soul and God, an affinity, a capacity in one for the other. Eckhart has numerous passages where he explores and expresses this idea, which for him is rooted in the Christian notion of creation. Of course, God is present to all creatures, by

[87]   McGinn 1986, 323.

virtue of his creating them, his sustaining them in being. But there is something unique about humanity: 'God said, "Let us make man in our image, after our likeness." ... So God created man in his own image, in the image of God he created him; male and female he created them.'[88] So human beings bear in themselves the image and likeness of God. And for Eckhart the 'image of God' is not a likeness in the way that one banana is like another banana, or one woman like another woman. This is not about two things which have something in common, because God and a human being are not 'two things', and they have nothing in common. The 'image of God' for Eckhart is God himself. For whatever is real in God must *be* God. If there is an image of God, then that image *is* God, uncreated and eternal. And of course, in biblical terms, that uncreated and eternal image of God is the Son, the second person of the Trinity, 'God from God, light from light, true God from true God'.[89] It is of this Son that Saint Paul writes: 'He is the image of the invisible God, the first-born of all creation. For in him all things were created in heaven and on earth, visible and invisible. He is before all things, and in him all things hold together.'[90] Christ is the image of God therefore, and he is God. Eckhart suggests that by making men and women 'in the image of God' God has made them in such a way that there is something uncreated and eternal at the heart of each human being. In each one of us there lies the Image. Here is Eckhart.

> How does a person come to be the only Son of the Father? Take note: The eternal Word did not take upon itself this person or that, but took upon itself one free, indivisible human nature, bare and without image ... And since in

[88] Genesis 1:26-7.
[89] This is the language of the Nicene Creed, a fundamental statement of Christian belief about Christ: *Deum de Deo, lumen de lumine, Deum verum de Deo vero*.
[90] Colossians 1:15-17.

this assumption the eternal Word took on human nature imagelessly, therefore the Father's Image, which is the eternal Son, became the image of human nature. ... Thus human nature was transformed by becoming the divine image, which is the image of the Father.[91]

God is in all things as being, as activity, as power. But he is fecund [i.e. 'gives birth'] only in the [human] soul; for though every creature is a vestige of God, the soul is the natural *image* of God. This image must be adorned and perfected in this birth. No creature but the soul alone is receptive to this act, this birth.[92]

This image is the Son of the Father, and I myself am this image, and this image is wisdom. .... Whoever does not understand, let him not worry.[93]

Eckhart has other language for the divine image in the human soul. He sometimes calls it 'the ground'. Commenting on Isaiah 45:15, 'Truly you are the hidden God', he reflects that God is hidden 'in the ground of the soul, where God's ground and the soul's ground are one ground'.[94] Here the distinction between God and the soul seems to have been dissolved. Does Eckhart maintain, as he was accused of doing by the inquisitors, that 'There is something in the soul that is uncreated and not capable of creation? Sometimes it might seem as if he was suggesting this. Here he is talking in the same way, but this time using the image of light:

Sometimes I have spoken of a light that is uncreated and not capable of creation, and it is in the soul. I always mention this light in my sermons, and this same light comprehends God without a medium, uncovered, naked,

[91]   Walshe 1979, ii, 27-8.
[92]   Walshe 1979, i, 15.
[93]   Walshe 1979, i, 121.
[94]   Colledge and McGinn 1986, 192.

as he is in himself; and this comprehension is to be understood as happening when the birth takes place. Here I may truly say that this light may have more unity with God than it has with any power of the soul, with which, however, it is one in being.[95]

One can see how the inquisitors might have found this kind of talk disturbing. If God is the Creator of all that exists, how can there be anything which exists which is uncreated? Eckhart's words seem to undermine the very notion of God as Creator. But perhaps it is possible to understand Eckhart in a way which does not do violence to the idea of Creation. What if the ground of the soul's being, the uncreated light, the uncreated image in the soul, is not 'something uncreated', but nothing? It is that dimension of the soul which is nothing, which is also the soul's *capacitas Dei* or 'capacity for God' as Augustine would have it – a God who is also Nothing.

> There is a power in the soul which is the intellect. ... Now St John says, "We shall be called children of God!" and if we are God's children we must resemble God. How is it then that a master says God is a being whom *nothing* is like? This is how you must understand it: By virtue of being like nothing, this power is like God. Just as God is like nothing, so too this power is like nothing.[96]

Throughout Eckhart's writings and sermons, what he insists on is that the soul must journey both into itself, into its own ground, and into God. And this is achieved by stripping away

---

[95]   Colledge and McGinn 1986, 198.

[96]   Walshe 1979, i, 296. Elsewhere he writes of this uncreated 'thing' in the soul: 'There is something in the soul in which God is bare, and the masters say this is nameless and has no name of its own. It is, and yet has no being of its own, for it is neither this nor that, nor here nor there.' (Walshe 1979, ii, 311)

everything. Just as we *speak* of God by stripping away images embedded in our language (apophatic theology), so we *enter* God by stripping away all that we have and are. We strip away all desire, all ideas, all images, all knowledge, to find the silence and nakedness and nothing which is the ground of our soul, which is where we meet God and become God.

> What should a person do who is to dwell in God? He should have three things. First that he has renounced himself and all things, and is not dependent on things which hold on to the senses from within; nor should he dwell on creatures that exist in time or eternity. Second he should not love *this* good or *that* good; he should love rather the Good from which all good flows. ... Thirdly, he should not take God as he is good or just; he should take him rather in that pure naked substance where he makes himself bare. Goodness and justice are pieces of clothing that cover God. Therefore strip everything from God that clothes him and take him bare in the dressing room where he is uncovered and naked in himself. Then you will truly remain in him ... When a person uncovers and lays bare the divine image that God created in him in creating his nature, then the image of God becomes visible ... Through the uncovering of his image in himself, this person becomes ever more similar to God because, by means of this image, a human being becomes more like God's image, the image that God is according to his bare being. The more a person lays himself bare, the more he is like God. And the more he is like God, the more he is united with God. [97]

In order to lay ourselves bare like this we must pursue absolute detachment. Not only from worldly wealth, pleasure, honours,

---

[97]   *Sermon* 40, McGinn 1986, 300.

respect, and so on. We must also strip ourselves of any will or desire of our own. We may not even have a desire for salvation, for if we love God in order to find salvation then we are seeking salvation rather than God, trying to *use* God in order to find something we want, for the satisfaction of our will. But we must strip ourselves of this will. We should not pray for things that we want, for if we do we will lose God, because our prayer is treating God as a means to an end. For Eckhart the process of stripping ourselves is so radical that we should cease to will anything, even willing to do the will of God.

> For I declare by the eternal truth, as long as you have a will to do the will of God, and a longing for eternity and God, you are not poor: for a poor man is one who wills nothing and desires nothing.[98]

We must become, or seek to become, nothing, for 'those who are equal to nothing, they alone are equal to God, for the divine being is equal to nothing, and in it there is neither image nor form.'[99] This also means that we should abandon all kinds of spiritual methods or techniques, or the quest for spiritual experience.

> When people think that they are acquiring more of God in inwardness, in devotion, in sweetness and various approaches than they do by the fireside or in the stable, you are acting just as if you took God and muffled his head up in a cloak and pushed him under a bench. Whoever seeks to find God by some way is finding a way and losing God.[100]
>
> Then how should I love God? You should love God unspiritually, that is, your soul should be unspiritual and

---

98   Walshe 1979, ii, 271.
99   Colledge and McGinn 1995, 187.
100   Colledge and McGinn 1995, 183.

stripped of all spirituality, for so long as your soul has a spirit's form it has images, and so long as it has images it has a medium, and so long as it has a medium it is not unity or simplicity. Therefore your soul must be unspiritual, free of all spirit, and must remain spiritless; for if you love God as he is God, as he is spirit, as he is person and as he is image – all this must go! Then how should I love him? You should love him as he is non-God, non-spirit, non-person, non-image, but as he is pure, unmixed, bright 'One', separated from all duality, and in that One we should eternally sink down, out of 'something' into 'nothing'. [101]

The soul must find and unite with God as Nothing by becoming nothing itself, and losing all its will and desire. Even the desire for God. This is something of a paradox. If the self-stripping of the soul is driven by the desire for God, then stripping oneself of such a desire is to defeat the purpose of the self-stripping in the first place. It leads to such paradoxes as Eckhart's cry: Therefore I pray to God to make me free of God, for my essential being is above God, taking God as the origin of creatures.'[102] This seems almost scandalous, but we must understand what Eckhart means by this. God as creator is God seen in his effects, or even as object (of desire), rather than God as he is in himself, the naked Ground, the One, or Nothing. As that Ground is also the Ground of Eckhart's naked soul, then in that sense Eckhart (the naked soul or Ground of Eckhart) is above 'God' conceived as creator.

I have done my best here to give a sympathetic account not only of Eckhart's view of God as Nothing but of his view of what a Christian life might look like. It is not always something I find attractive or convincing: his emphasis on the intellect, the weight he gives to detachment from the love of all things, and the priority of detachment over love, are all aspects which give

[101]   Colledge and McGinn 1995, 208.
[102]   Walshe 1979, ii, 274.

me misgivings. Furthermore, his presentation of detachment as the 'way' to God seems incompatible with his principled objection to using any kind of 'way' ('Whoever seeks a way to God will find a way and lose God'). Nevertheless, his exploration of the Nothingness of God is profound and compelling. And difficult though the path of detachment may be, who would not be stirred by his invitation? 'Therefore stand still, and do not waver before your emptiness.'[103]

---

[103]   Walshe 1979 , i, 44.

CHAPTER NINE.

MODERN PHILOSOPHERS: HEGEL, FEUERBACH, MARX

THE QUESTION OF 'God' has haunted modern philosophy in countless ways. Unlike the medieval world, modern thought has *not* simply assumed that 'God exists', or that prayer is meaningful, or that we are 'created', or that we have some eternal purpose. When you are sitting with ten people in a pub you can't assume that any of them find any meaning in talk about 'God' – a very different scenario from that of Aquinas's time, when you could assume that they *all* did.

By modern philosophy, I mean philosophy of the nineteenth and twentieth centuries, some of the thinkers who have left their stamp on the way we think in the modern world today. I am not going to give a full account, or even a broad general account of *any* of these three philosophers' works – Hegel, Feuerbach and Marx. I'm not a philosopher of any sort, and my grasp of modern philosophy is pretty minimal. What I want to do is simply to identify parts of their works where the idea of 'God as Nothing' might have some relevance, and to look at what kind of relevance it might actually have. It is, if you like, a kind of taster or experiment – wondering how the idea of God as Nothing might shape our response to some aspects of modern thought.

Our discussion in some of the earlier chapters has been partly concerned with metaphysics, with what you might call abstract questions of being: what does it mean for something to exist? What is it for something to be this kind of thing rather than that kind of thing, to be an individual being? and so on.

Much modern philosophy, however, has gone in quite different directions, abandoning much of the metaphysical discussion. Modern philosophers have been inclined to have quite different centres of interest: politics or political economy, for example; or the nature and workings of language. Take Karl Marx, for example. Few philosophers have had such an international impact, and been so quoted as an authority for so many different things. Few philosophers, if any, have had their works so ceaselessly read not just by other philosophers, but by revolutionaries, by tyrants, by government bureaucrats and ideologues, and by social critics of one sort and another. Few philosophers have had their ideas so fully incorporated into the background assumptions of modern thought.

Let us ask if Dr Marx can shed any light on the question of God as Nothing, or vice versa for that matter. But first we might just note that if you were to ask people to name one atheist philosopher – not just a philosopher who happens to be an atheist, but a philosopher for whom atheism is a fundamental tenet of his philosophy – it is likely that Karl Marx would be one of the most frequently named. His philosophy makes an issue of atheism, and political regimes which have (at least nominally) promoted Marxist philosophy have been notable for their hostility to 'religious' belief and practice.

Why is Marx regarded as an atheist – apart from the obvious reason that he didn't believe in God, and regarded all religion as a form of 'false consciousness'? Perhaps a better way of asking the question is to ask what did Marx *mean* by his atheism? What was it for? Where did it come from? How did it fit into other aspects of his thought?

Marx's notion of dialectical materialism – his philosophical method in which atheism appears to be so significant – embodies two philosophical ideas which he inherited from other thinkers. One idea was dialectic, which he inherited from Hegel. The other idea was materialism, which he inherited from someone else, as we'll see shortly. But let's look at dialectic first of all. It was the contribution of Georg Wilhelm Friedrich Hegel (1770-1831). For Hegel, human history was the history of ideas. It was a history of progress: an abstract idea may be held, but it will be challenged by a different idea, by a contradiction within its own expression, or by other ideas, or the facts on the ground and human experience. The initial idea is thus negated by another idea, and a new third idea is hammered out – thesis, antithesis and synthesis. Hegel's concept of *Aufhebung* refers to the nullification or 'overcoming' of both the original idea and its contradiction, as a new idea or synthesis replaces it, though elements of both the thesis and its antithesis may remain in some transformed state in the new synthesis. Thus humanity, or at least humanity's thinking and understanding, is seen as pushing forward into the future. It is an image of progress, inching step-by-step towards some future goal of perfect understanding, of freedom from conflict, and so on. As ideas got better, of course, people would understand things better, and as they understood things better, if they put their ideas and understanding into practice, they could make the world better too.

Hegel's dialectic of ideas provided the dialectical part of Marx's 'dialectical materialism'. Hegel, incidentally, did 'believe in God'. He remained a Lutheran of some sort throughout his life, though not all Lutherans liked the implications of his work. While denying that God was a 'being' among others, he seemed to see God as some idea that people were working their way towards, the forwards-projection of the dialectics of the human mind and experience, something that arises out of ourselves.

So Hegel contributed the dialectic to Karl Marx's thinking. What about the materialism? This was very much the contribution of a man called Ludwig Feuerbach, another nineteenth-century German, a former Hegelian who 'stood Hegel on his head'. For Feuerbach, the world was not about ideas, which is how he regarded Hegel's view. For Feuerbach, the reality was not ideas but real human beings, bodily creatures living in bodily relationships with each other and with the material world around them. This is what he means by 'materialism'. The essence of humanity is not a dialectic of ideas, as Hegel said, but is simply the fact that we are what we are, what we see around us. Nature, existing independent of ideas and philosophy, is what it is, and we human beings are ourselves products of nature. And nothing exists outside of nature and man. All the religious ideas we have are simply what he calls 'the fantastic reflection of our own essence'. What religious people worship, for Feuerbach, is simply an objectification – an unreal objectification – of our own nature and our own sense of what is good. In the end, Feuerbach says, he ended up believing only in man: 'God was my first thought; reason, my second; and man, my third and last'. He started off as a religious believer, but under the influence of Hegel he then believed in reason, the advance of ideas (and God became merely part of that, the most sublime 'idea' of all); and finally he threw it all over, and believed only in Man. Man was the centre of the universe, the ultimate being. God was merely a fantasy.

What Marx did was to take the confrontation of Feuerbach's materialism and Hegel's dialectic idealism, and give birth to Dialectical Materialism. Marx believes in the progress of dialectic, the appearing of contradictions, their resolution or *Aufhebung*, and the movement on to the next and higher stage. But these contradictions are not contradictions between ideas, theories or beliefs, as Hegel thought. For Marx the contradictions are rather in the material ways in which men and women live their lives, the contradictions embedded in economic activity, between human needs and human resources; contradictions between power and powerlessness, and above all contradictions between social classes. The progressive force of dialectic is taken out of our philosophical heads, and put onto the streets, into factories, into our existence in the natural world, into people's daily lives and their economic circumstances. In this sense it becomes materialist. Where Feuerbach had placed man at the centre and thought that mankind would be liberated by love, Marx and his colleague Engels agreed with his placing humanity in the centre, but complained that Feuerbach put 'literary phrases in the place of scientific knowledge, the liberation of mankind by means of "love" in place of the emancipation of the proletariat through the economic transformation of production'.

So Marx seems to have accepted Feuerbach's rejection of God. For Feuerbach it was human beings who were important, not God or ideas. He dethroned God, you might say, and made Man the centre of the world, and the centre of Marx's thinking. Whatever diminished the centrality and priority of Man, he said, was to be cast aside. Man alone was what counted.

For Feuerbach this meant asserting atheism. For Feuerbach, God and Man were two beings, and they were in competition with each other, each demanding to be placed at the centre of meaning. When you consider what really matters it has to be seen as *either* divine *or* human. If you see God as the centre of meaning, you diminish the human, because you are putting God above humanity. If you see the centre as human, then you must cast aside the divine. You have to choose: either God or humanity must be at the centre of the world of meaning and value. Whatever you give to God, Feuerbach says, is stolen from humanity. To make a full and whole-hearted option for humanity, you must abandon God. If you are a humanist you must reject God; and if you are religious you will reject Man.

Now this Feuerbachian dilemma rests on one fundamental view of God. It rests on the view that God is something. It implies that God and Man can be listed alongside each other as two potential centres of our attention; as competing entities, only one of which we can accept. As the Hegel scholar Quentin Lauer said: 'There is no conceivable God that would be acceptable, for any being in any way superior to man is simply inconceivable.' This is what Feuerbach believes, and in some ways Marx follows him. The insistence on putting humanity at the centre of history, this materialist conception of history, implies getting rid of God. If God and humanity are rivals, only one can be at the centre.

And this would be true, surely, if God and humanity were two different beings. If there were two entities, God and humanity, in competition for our attention and service, then to serve God would be to treat humanity as less than absolute; it would be to put our fellow men and women on the periphery of our attention. If there were a shared space occupied by God and humanity within which God could be measured or evaluated and found to be 'superior to man' (in Lauer's phrase), then we would be forced to choose: are we going to put loving God at the centre of our lives, or loving our fellow men and women?

But as we have seen, God is not any kind of thing; and God does not occupy any common space with human beings where they might be rivals. For two things to be rivals, and for us to have to choose between them, they must have something in common. We can choose between a circle and a square, because they are two shapes. We can choose between a sheep and a goat, because they are two animals. But God and man are not two kinds of anything. God is not any kind of anything, and so we can't really choose between having God at the centre of our vision or having man at the centre. We don't have to choose between loving God and loving our neighbour; on the contrary, each is an expression of the other.

175

Let's read that sentence by Lauer again, expressing Feuerbach's (and later Marx's) materialist view: 'There is no conceivable God that would be acceptable, for any being in any way superior to man is simply inconceivable.' Whatever this means, it cannot refer to the Christian meaning of the word 'God' – at least not if what I have been saying for the last eight chapters is true. Christians don't believe in a 'conceivable God'. And whatever the word 'God' does mean for Christians, it cannot mean 'a being superior to man' in the sense intended here. Something is superior to something else only if they can be measured on the same scale. A horse is bigger than a sheep, only because they can both be measured on the scale of feet and inches. A trumpet is louder than a harp, only because they can both be measured on the scale of decibels. A centipede has more feet than a cat, only because their feet can both be counted on the conventional scale of numbers. You can only compare things and find one superior to another if they have something in common to begin with. But God and man have nothing in common, not even that they are both existing beings. God cannot be compared to anything; nothing can be compared to God. So the 'God' that Lauer can't accept, who is 'conceivable' and 'superior to man', is not the God of Judaeo-Christian faith. And it follows that even if we want to celebrate and centre humanity, there is no need to reject God, because they simply aren't in competition, and they can't be.

Now Feuerbach and Marx simply never addressed the ancient and orthodox tradition, in either Jewish or Christian theology, of God as Nothing. They show no sign of even being aware of it. In a display of rather impressive ignorance, Feuerbach in particular repeatedly insists (against all the evidence of the theological tradition) that Christians think that they know what God is, that God is an individual existing being, and that he is conceivable, that we know what he is and what is attributes are. Here is what he says in his work *The Essence of Christianity*:

> Where man removes all determinations from God, God is reduced to a negative being, to a being that is not a being. To a truly religious man, however, God is not a being without determinations, because he is a definite, real being to him. Hence, the view that God is without determinations, that he cannot be known, is a product of the modern era, of modern unbelief (§2).

Well we have seen that a God without determinations – that is, a God who is beyond description, beyond the limits of language – is not a 'product of the modern era', but goes right back into the Hebrew tradition, and is a constant, an idea simply assumed by medieval Christian theologians like Thomas Aquinas, and by Jewish theologians like Rabbi Moses.

Now the question I'd like to ask Marx is this: did he really accept Feuerbach's assumption as much as he seemed to? Generally speaking it seems that he did. The assertion of humanity as the centre of all meaning is constantly stressed, and it is simply *assumed* that this means 'dethroning God'. For Marx, God is an 'alien power', something over against man, and if man is to be emancipated he must be emancipated from God.

That is why in Marx's vision of the future classless society, there is no room at all for religion. Religion will simply disappear. Marx can envision all kinds of ideologies which exist now, which *will* continue to exist in the future – albeit in a transformed way, freed from all the distortion and alienation which they suffer from in this class society where we live. So in the future there will continue to be art and music, there will be law and politics and philosophy, in the new world. They will be purified of all the bourgeois features which now distort them, but they will be there in a new way, liberated from their old enslavement to class interests. But religion won't be there. Religion is the one ideology which won't exist, which is incapable of redemption. And that is because, following

Feuerbach, Marx sees God entirely as a feature of our present alienation, an 'alien power' which forces man into second place, which prevents man from finding freedom. (It should be said that the idea of 'alien power' in Marx's thought applies in the first instance to 'man himself' rather than God or gods. The worker's labour is alienated by the system in which he works so that it becomes wealth he creates *over against* himself, hostile to him because it is taken by another; that is for Marx the 'alien power'. God appears as a mark of alienation, therefore, as a kind of 'theologised' account of the human experience of alienation, which is essentially economic, political, social.)

As we have seen, the tradition of God as Nothing can help us to answer Marx. To say that the world is created, to say that God loves the world into being for example, to say that God makes Man his own image, male and female, is *not* to say that Man is marginal. It doesn't put humanity in second place, because God and humanity are not and cannot be rivals.

And strangely there is one place where it seems to me that Marx almost recognizes this. He has this to say about atheism, in a way which decisively rejects the Feuerbachian rivalry of God and humanity. Marx wants simply to opt for humanity, and denies any need for atheism. In a sense, Marx is denying that he is an atheist – which will be a pretty surprising state of affairs for most folk who know anything about Marx:

> Atheism, as a denial of this unreality (i.e. belief in God) is no longer meaningful, for atheism is the negation of God and seeks to assert by this negation the existence of man. Socialism no longer requires such a roundabout method. ... It is positive human self-consciousness, no longer a self-consciousness attained through the negation of religion.[104]

---

[104] *Economic and Philosophical Manuscripts* (1844), in Bottomore 1975, 166-7).

Here we find Marx abolishing the need for atheism. Atheism, he says, 'is no longer meaningful.' He doesn't accept that asserting the existence of man requires us to deny the existence of God. For Feuerbach you assert the essence and existence of man, the centrality of mankind, by denying God, because they are in competition. But in this passage Marx seems to reject the competition between man and God, the contradiction. There is no antithesis between God and man. Feuerbach's view of man is still in some ways an abstract one. It is an idea, based on the denial of God. But Marx says, never mind God. Never mind asserting or denying God. Just look at the way men and women live their lives, the structures of power and wealth in which they have to live, and the alienation that this produces. It is in resistance to an 'alien power' that we see the assertion of humanity, and there is no need to deny God in order to assert humanity. To get there by denying God is simply to treat humanity as an abstract, the opposite of which is God. But these are not opposite abstractions. Humanity is real, made up of observable and understandable individuals in their own concrete material existence. Go out and have a look.

So Marx, at least at this point in his writings, has moved beyond the God vs. humanity competition. He doesn't see God as something else, another being, which reduces human freedom or autonomy. For Marx, at least in this paragraph, there is no need to deny God by atheism. All that is necessary is to assert the human. A Christian might very well agree and cite Galatians 5:14 to that effect: 'For the entire law is fulfilled in keeping this one command: "Love your neighbour as yourself."' Everything that is required of us is that we attend to one another, to the human. Asserting or denying gods, any being which might limit human flourishing, is not our task.

Or we might put it this way: Marx's critique of 'God' is more or less indistinguishable from Christian critique of 'gods'.

CHAPTER TEN.

GOD AND THE POETS: R. S. THOMAS AND PAUL CELAN

THE IDEA OF God as Nothing can be explored in poetry too. Normally when we speak of theology we think of something systematic, and – at least when done properly – rational, analytic. It constructs propositions and it criticises (or deconstructs) propositions. It tests and challenges the language of 'God-talk'. It is (at its best) capable of rational discussion, capable of commanding assent or provoking dissent. But poetry does not normally behave like that. It depends on sound - rhythm and rhyme, assonance, alliteration, and (at least on the printed page) on visual clues like line-breaks and spaces. Poetry may also play with the juxtaposition of alien images and elements, opening up strange ways of seeing through its own reinventions of language. This may be theology too, if it is talk about God, but it is a rather different way of talking, and it summons a different kind of response.

If all our religious language is groping towards the Nothing we call 'God', it is perhaps most articulate at the very moment when it breaks down in the face of sheer unknowability. As one of the poets in this chapter says:

> *Wittgenstein's signposts pointing*
> *at the boundaries of language*
> *into the obligatory void.* (R. S. Thomas, 'Markers')

In this sense theological prose is most powerful when it reveals itself as inadequate, but is there perhaps something about poetry, which moves beyond the measured analysis and control of prose, which opens cracks in the imagination? 'There is a crack in everything,' Leonard Cohen sang, 'That's how the light gets in.'[105]

Is that not why, when we go to church, we don't simply sit and discuss and analyse ideas. We sing – poetry set to music. And the song's power is its power to change the singer. As Matthew Arnold wrote, 'Such a price the gods exact for song: to become what we sing.'

What we will do in this chapter is to look briefly at two very different poets. Perhaps having read this chapter you will want to read them both in more depth, at greater length. But here we will merely draw out this one thread from the broad and complex world created by each poet: the way each of them touches on our theme of God as Nothing.

The two poets are both twentieth-century characters. R. S. Thomas was a Welshman, a Christian (and an Anglican priest); Paul Celan was a Romanian Jew. These men have various things in common, apart from some rather interesting issues about how we use the word 'God'. They are both poets who wrote in languages which were problematic for them. R. S. Thomas wrote in English. That was his mother tongue, but it was the language of a nation that he felt had betrayed and oppressed his beloved Wales and the Welsh language. English was the language,

---

[105] Leonard Cohen, 'Anthem', 1984.

indeed, of his mother, whom he describes as being rather snobbish about such things, imagining her English language made her superior to Welsh-speakers. Thomas sees the English language as part of a history of cultural extermination from the arrival of the Anglo-Normans in Wales onwards, undermining Welsh culture, identity, history and spirituality. But English is his language, nevertheless. He did learn Welsh and wrote some Welsh prose, but all his published poems, except for one, are in English. So he laments these English forces on Wales, and regrets his involvement with them, and the fact that –awful imagery! – even the poetry he vomits out contains his mother's poison:

> ... *I was*
> *born into the squalor of*
> *their feeding and sucked their speech*
> *in with my mother's*
> *infected milk, so that whatever*
> *I throw up now is still theirs.*[106]

Paul Celan also had a problem with the language in which he wrote. He was originally Paul Antschel, but he re-named himself after the war, turning his name upside down – perhaps a gesture towards that overturning of language which was central to his idea of poetry. He was born in 1920 in Czernowitz (then part of northern Romania, but absorbed into Ukraine after the Second World War), into a middle-class German-speaking Jewish family. For his mother in particular, German was the language of culture, of thought and literature. She tended to be more of an assimilationist than his father, as many middle-class Jews of the period were, and this was something he inherited from her. German was his mother-tongue, so writing and speaking in German

---

[106]   'It Hurts him to Think', Thomas 1993, 262.

bonded him to her and her ideas, her ways of talking and thinking, her way of seeing the world. But Celan's parents were taken by the Germans when Czernowitz was under German control, before the Soviets occupied it in 1943. They both died in concentration camps, and Paul himself spent a year in a forced labour camp. The deaths of his parents, the deaths of his loved ones, and so many others, were overwhelming. His poetry and his life thereafter are shaped by 'that which happened' – his term for what is unspeakable, the millions of deaths in the industrial killing-machine of the Third Reich. His mother, shot as 'unfit for work' in 1942 in a prison camp in Transnistria, is a constant haunting presence, often the *du* or 'you' addressed in his poems:

> *It's falling, Mother, snow in the Ukraine:*
> *The Saviour's crown a thousand grains of grief.*
> *Here all my tears reach out to you in vain.*
> *One proud mute glance is all of my relief...*[107]

He also allows his mother's voice to speak to him in his verse:

> *... Oh for a cloth, child,*
> *to wrap myself in when it's flashing with helmets,*
> *when the rosy floe bursts, when snowdrift sifts your father's*
> *bones, hooves crushing*
> *the Song of the Cedar.*[108]

His mother-tongue and his struggle with it is fundamental to his poetry. How to speak in his mother's language which was also the language of the people who killed his mother? As John Felstiner says in his wonderful study of Celan's work (*Paul Celan: Poet, Survivor, Jew*):

---

[107]   Felstiner 1995, 17.
[108]   Felstiner 1995, 18.

Celan's lyrics, being in German, pose a particular challenge. For the Thousand-Year-Reich organized its genocide of European Jewry by means of language: slogans, slurs, pseudo-scientific dogma, propaganda, euphemism, and the jargon that brought about every devastating 'action', from the earliest racial 'laws' through 'special treatment' in the camps to the last 'resettlement' of Jewish orphans. Celan has become an exemplary postwar poet because he insistently registered in German the catastrophe made in Germany. With his world obliterated, he held fast to the mother tongue that was both his and the murderers' ... Insofar as it was language that had been damaged, his verse might repair the damage.[109]

So both these poets are alert to the difficulties of the languages in which they write. Thomas writes about his beloved Wales in English, the language he thinks has destroyed his people's culture. Celan writes in German which was, as he said, his *Muttersprache und Mördersprache* – both his mother-tongue (and his mother's tongue) and the language of the murderers, the German Reich which murdered his family.

But there are other difficulties with language. For both these poets, language collapses on itself in some way when faced with a mystery that is beyond naming. And in each case this collapse of language takes place in the most dramatic way in the attempt to speak about God.

R. S. Thomas, the Anglican priest, served in various parishes in Wales. He was inspired by Welshness, or at least by his view of Welshness and its connection to the hard wild landscape that he loved, and to the communities that he served. All this shapes his poetry, but at the heart of it is the larger question of 'God'. Richard McLauchlan's brilliant study of Thomas's writings, *Saturday's Silence*, explores that question in

[109] Felstiner 1995, xvii.

depth.[110] The title picks up a theme rooted in the chronology of the Gospels: the death of Christ on Good Friday, his silence in the tomb on Saturday, and his resurrection on Easter Sunday. In this time-picture we are those who dwell in the Silence of Saturday. As George Steiner wrote in the conclusion of his essay *Real Presences*:

> Ours is the long day's journey of the Saturday. Between suffering, aloneness, unutterable waste on the one hand and the dream of liberation, of rebirth on the other. In the face of the torture of a child, of the death of love which is Friday, even the greatest art and poetry are almost helpless. In the Utopia of the Sunday, the aesthetic will, presumably, no longer have logic or necessity.[111]

In this scheme, Saturday is where we live. We look back at Friday's catastrophe, the destruction of all meaning and sense, but we live in hope as we struggle to mend the world and find (or make) meaning. We may not anticipate a utopian Sunday, the rebirth and renewal of life, in some glib, optimistic certainty. That would be a cheap and easy grace. Instead we dwell between those two days, conscious of Friday's horror, but still in hope, even if we are unable to say what we hope for or how it will come. As Augustine says, 'It is longing that makes the heart grow deep.'

McLauchlan argues that Christ, God's Word made flesh, is spoken in time. On Friday that Word cries out in abandonment, 'Why have you forsaken me?' On Saturday that Word is reduced to the silence of the tomb. The incarnate Word of God, destroyed on Friday, on Saturday is absent. But because this is the Word of God, even that silence is God's self-revelation, and even that absence is where God is. The word

[110]   Richard McLauchlan, *Saturday's Silence: R.S. Thomas and Paschal Reading* (Cardiff, 2016).
[111]   Steiner 1989, 232.

that God speaks on Saturday is the silence into which Christ has entered. His people must follow him into that abyss, and part of that following is our own silence and (when and if we speak) the failure of our speech. Just as for Eckhart we find the nothingness of God by becoming nothing ourselves, so for Thomas we encounter the silence of God by becoming silent ourselves. (Interestingly, Thomas once said that he had found reading Eckhart 'an eye-opener'.)

So Thomas is constantly concerned with the failure of speech. In his poem 'The Gap' we see humans building a tower of language (think of the Tower of Babel) to reach up to God:

> God woke, but the nightmare
> did not recede. Word by Word
> the tower of speech grew.
> He looked at it from the air
> he reclined on. One word more and
> it would be on a level
> with him; vocabulary would have triumphed.

But human language is not adequate to the task, and cannot reach God. In the poem 'there was the blank still by his name', a blank space in language, an absence, a darkness, and so God himself makes 'the sign in the space' with 'the darkness that is a god's blood'. No mere language can cross this darkness. It is:

> the narrowness that we stare
> over into the eternal
> silence that is the repose of God.

The silence of God is quite properly echoed by the silence of humanity. In his early poem 'In a Country Church', even in prayer it is silence that is our place of revelation.

> *To one kneeling down no word came,*
> *Only the wind's song, saddening the lips*
> *Of the grave saints, rigid in glass ...*

In 'The Letter' we find the same movement from language to silence. It begins:

> *I look up from my book*
> *from the unreality of language,*
> *and stare at the sea's surface*
> *that says nothing and means it.*

In the end however, as he stares silently at the sea, the 'nothing' of its surface is replaced with the nothing of its 'concealed fathoms', a 'superficial nothing' gives way to a 'deep nothing' we might say:

> *... I gaze myself into accepting*
> *that to pray true is to say nothing.*

The failure of language then leads us to silence, but this is God's silence, and God reaches through his silence to reveal himself beyond language, beyond knowledge. Thus in the poem 'In a Country Church' he reveals himself not as something called God, but in the poet's gaze at something quite other:

> *Was he balked by silence? He kneeled long,*
> *And saw love in a dark crown*
> *Of thorns blazing, and a winter tree*
> *Golden with fruit of a man's body.*

There is a vision, but it is a vision of nothing, or a vision of things which are not God. In the great list of things which are available for vision, God is not on the list.

Just as silence is the not-language, the not-speech, in

187

which we encounter God, so our encounter with God is the encounter with Nothing, a not-presence, an absence. In 'Via Negativa' any seeking for God as a 'someone' or a 'something' fails completely.

Why no! I never thought other than
That God is that great absence
In our lives, the empty silence
Within, the place where we go
Seeking, not in hope to
Arrive or find. He keeps the interstices
In our knowledge, the darkness
Between stars. His are the echoes
We follow, the footprints he has just
Left. We put our hands in
His side hoping to find
It warm. We look at people
And places as though he had looked
At them, too; but miss the reflection.

Nothing is encountered. And perhaps we didn't even hope to encounter anything, because we know that God is Nothing – 'we go seeking not in hope to arrive or find'. When we look into the night sky we may see stars, but 'He' is the darkness between the stars where there is nothing. We may see a footprint, but that is merely the mark of someone who is not there, someone who has gone. The question of seeing becomes not whether or not we can see God, but whether or not we can see as God sees, 'to look at people and places as though he had looked at them', to know and love people, creatures, as God knows and loves them, whatever that might mean. There is no 'Being' here, but only a highly charged absence. Once the idea of God as a particular being has been abandoned, once you have embraced the absence or the 'Nothing' which is, for Thomas, the experience of God, then you can enter into your own emptiness and silence, the 'Saturday's Silence' which is God's self-revelation. There is no 'finding of God', because there is nothing to find. We cannot encounter the divine as an object we can attend to. We encounter the divine not when we attend to something called God (because there is Nothing called God) but when we attend to 'people and places', and then we are joined to God not by seeing God, but by seeing *them*. And those last four words: 'but (we) miss the reflection'. What we miss is the reflection of God. He has looked at them, these people and places, and we might hope that by looking at them we might catch a reflection of God. But we don't. We miss the reflection. God has already left. God is absent, or absence.

There are other poems we might explore in this way. One called 'Hesitations', where again the poet seems to be on a quest for God:

> *Old gods are no good;*
> *they are smaller than*
> *they promise, or else they are large*
> *like mountains, leaning over*
> *the soul to admire themselves.*

'Old gods are no good', because they are beings, individuals, either too small and petty to be of interest, or so vast that they overwhelm all human value or meaning – a bit like the 'God' rejected by Feuerbach, you will remember, who demanded our attention at the expense of humanity. The poet comes to towns (perhaps the shallow shopping centres full of the useless industry and consumption which he despised) and he says:

> *No God there. I would have*
> *passed on, but a music*
> *detained me in one of*
> *blood flowing, where two*

people side by side
under the arc lamps
lay, from one to the other.

Again, there is 'no God there', no god to be found as an individual being, as an object of discovery. The poet is 'detained' not by something called 'God' but by 'a music' present in two people lying together, two human bodies. It is as if he senses not the presence of any existing 'being', but a dimension ('a music') of the things which do exist.

Thomas is a Christian, and a priest, and readers might be surprised by the way his poetry explores silence and emptiness and the absence of gods. Many who have not thought carefully about the Jewish and Christian rejection of an individual called 'God' might even suggest that this was a loss of faith. Is this merely atheism? It may appear so if we think of 'God' as the name of an individual entity, and we may consider that Thomas's rejection of gods and 'God' is an atheist moment.

But such 'atheism' is not the opposite of faith (idolatry, not atheism, is the opposite of faith); it is rather a part of faith. Atheism is the denial of the existence of any individual entity called 'God' or of any entities called 'gods'; but faith does not assert the existence of such an entity. Instead atheism is part of a process in which the mind is freed from the tyranny of 'the old gods' and from the bewitching notion of some super-God as an existing individual. Perhaps we should even see such atheism as a *necessary* part of faith for believers who love in this 'Saturday' condition. Thomas makes no assertion of 'a being' but waits in the empty silence around him ('In Church'), where there is no sound but his breath:

... There is no other sound
In the darkness but the sound of a man
Breathing, testing his faith

On emptiness, nailing his questions
One by one to an untenanted cross.

The abolition of the gods – a kind of atheism – far from expressing a loss of faith, is the work of a most profound believer working through the experience of God as Nothing, as 'emptiness'. There is no God who might be 'found' or be the object of experience. It is rather as he says in another poem ('Kneeling'): 'the meaning is in the waiting'. If all his seeking and waiting were to result in an encounter with 'something' or 'someone', he would surely turn away muttering 'not this, not this', because his belief is not in such and such a thing. Because this is still the Saturday of 'emptiness', of the 'untenanted cross'.

The cross, whether tenanted (on Friday) or untenanted (on Saturday) remains at the heart of the poet's vision. This cross is the 'something' – a historical something, an actual event – that we can look towards in our quest for the silent Nothing which is God. In 'Contacts':

The scholar bends over
his book and the sage his navel
to enter the labyrinthine
mind and find at the centre the axis
on which it spins. But for the one
who is homeless
there is only the tree with the body
on it, eternally convulsed
by the shock of its contact
with the exposed nerve of love.

Words and reason and our own meditations fail us – whether scholar or sage – and we must strip ourselves and become 'homeless', unhoused as our language-shelter crumbles, and look back from our current place of silence to Friday's 'tree' bearing its tortured body. And perhaps only in that last line is

191

there some faint foreshadowing of hope: 'the exposed nerve of love' revealed in Friday's convulsed body offers also the faintest promise of the healing encounter of Sunday, though what such an encounter might mean, and with what, remains unknown.

৯৪

Let's move on now to our other poet, Paul Celan. Celan had grown up with an Orthodox Jewish father, apparently something of a bully and rather distant from his son, and his more gentle mother. Unlike Thomas, Celan was dealing with his own God-question in the very specific historical context of the Holocaust. It was not only a great atrocity of the twentieth century, but a personal catastrophe for him. After the destruction of his parents, his family, the whole world of European Jews – and of course, the destruction of all the *meaning* that was embedded in that world – what could the word 'God' mean in a context like that?

This question haunted believers – and not only Jews – for the rest of the twentieth century. Some lost their faith altogether, while some deepened their faith with layers of reflection on suffering and loss. Others developed a whole new theology of destruction and redemption, which sometimes left them with rather problematic views of God such as the view that the state of Israel is so *theologically* necessary that it is permissible to do evil in order to defend it.

Celan developed a different response, far more complex, contradictory. His poetry constantly reaches out to speak to someone, to re-establish communication and, with communication, meaning. The German word *du*, 'you', appears over and over again in his work – poetry addressed to *du*. It is the more informal or intimate word for 'you', as distinct from the more formal *sie*. Celan uses the word 1,300 times and many, perhaps most, of his poems are addressed to some 'you'. We must surely see here the influence of the Austrian

Jewish writer Martin Buber (1878-1965). Celan adored Buber, so much so that in 1960, when the seventy-two-year-old Buber came to a hotel in Paris where Celan was living, the poet called on him and knelt at his feet to ask for his blessing. Buber's 1923 book *Ich und Du* ('I and Thou') had proposed that humans find their meaning in relationship, when we treat another person not merely as 'object' – as an 'it' – but by treating her as 'Thou', as relational. In a book on Buber that he bought in 1959 Celan underlined these words: 'Creatures stand within the secret of Creation, of Speech ... We can say "Thou", because "Thou" is also said to us. ... Spirit is not in the I, but between I and Thou'.[112]

It is this quest for a *du*, 'thou' or 'you', that provides the emotional energy for Celan's poetry. As Felstiner notes, this *du* in his poems could be addressed to 'himself, his mother, wife or sons, a loved one or a friend, the Jewish dead, their God, Nelly Sachs, Rembrandt, Rosa Luxemburg, Saint Francis of Assisi, Rabbi Loew of Prague, King Lear, a plant, a stone, a word, the Word, or the Hebrew letter *Bet* or to something indeterminable, present only because the speaker calls it *du*.'[113] It's not always clear who this *du* is, but this reaching out to the other is a constant in his poetry, a quest to realise his own humanity and to find meaning in relationship. So in the forced labour of the Nazi camps:

THERE WAS EARTH INSIDE THEM, and
they dug.

They dug and they dug, so their day
went by for them, their night. And they did not praise God,
who, so they heard, wanted all this,
who, so they heard, knew all this.

---

[112]   Felstiner 1995, 140.
[113]   Felstiner 1995, xvi.

They dug and heard nothing more;
they did not grow wise, invented no song,
thought up for themselves no language.
They dug.

There came a stillness, and there came a storm,
and all the oceans came.
I dig, you dig, and the worm digs too,
and that singing out there says: They dig.

O one, o none, o no one, o you
[O einer, o keiner, o niemand, o du]:
Where did the way lead when it led nowhere?
O you dig and I dig, and I dig towards you,
and on our finger the ring awakes.[114]

'God' appears here in the first verse, but not a god worthy of praise; and they did not praise him. He was a 'god', so they heard, who knew and wanted all this. He is discussed in the third person as a 'he' – the object in Buber's 'I-it' scheme – and rejected. But there is also a *du* who is addressed in the last verse of the poem who is clearly not the 'God' of the first verse. In the final verse there is a 'one' (*einer*) who is 'no one' (*niemand*) and who is the *du* addressed directly by the poet. And as the poet digs towards this *du*, the *du* also digs – perhaps toward the poet, or perhaps alongside the poet, sharing that toil. Not a *du* who 'wills all this', but who suffers it alongside the poet, or even in the poet. And of course the poem itself, like most of his poems, could be seen as Celan's digging towards this *du*, and in digging reaching out to some union with *niemand*, with 'no one'. Like R. S. Thomas in his Saturday of silence and waiting, Celan reaches out towards a *du* of which he cannot take hold. Digging, waiting, calling out do not come to a satisfactory

[114] Celan 1996, 157.

194

ending. There is no solution. There is simply 'no one' to whom he must reach out, on whom he must call, towards whom he must dig.

There is much of Celan's poetry which is not *about* the holocaust, but there is little of his work that is not haunted by that experience in some way. And the continuous use of *du,* 'thou', reflects part of that haunting. It is the need of the poet to reach out and make contact, to 'encounter', as he often said. Out of the isolation of loss and pain, he says, 'I went with my very being toward language ... there would have to be readers again ... after what had happened'. Thus his reader is also *du* for Celan. Only by making contact, 'a handshake' or a 'handgrasp' as he called it, can we find meaning in the destruction of meaning that was the great extermination.

This means the poet stretching out his hand, reaching out to his readers of course; but also for Celan reaching out to his mother, his father, to those who were lost, and perhaps also to God – but the God who is nothing. The God who *did* nothing during the Holocaust, and who says (or said) nothing. Celan speaks to this silence (as *du*) over and over again in several of his poems. In his 'Conversation in the Mountains', the name of this silence is turned into a question, 'HearestThou' (*HörstDu*). 'Says he, says he ... You hear, he says ... And HearestThou, of course, HearestThou, he says nothing, he doesn't answer, because HearestThou, that's the one with the glaciers ...'[115] The icy silence of a nameless One, a No-One whose very name has become a question, and who said nothing when 'One evening the sun, and not only that, had gone down'. How many millions of agonies are concealed below the surface of 'not only that' – an evil that cannot be named, which is simply 'that which happened'.

Perhaps we may compare the refusal to name the great evil with the typical Jewish refusal to name God. Celan certainly

---

[115]   Felstiner 1995, 143

took this second refusal seriously. He made numerous annotations in his copy of an essay by Hugo Bergmann, 'The Sanctification of the Name', marking many sentences and writing at the very beginning the Hebrew words of Leviticus 22:31-2: 'And ye shall keep my commandments, and do them. I am the Lord. And ye shall not profane My holy name but I will be sanctified among the children of Israel. I am the Lord who sanctifies you.' The Hebrew word here translated as 'the Lord' is the four-letter unspeakable name YHWH (יהוה). When it is encountered in a text, the reader says *Adonai*, 'the Lord', instead of reading it as it is written. (God may also be referred to tangentially in Hebrew as *Ha Shem* 'The Name', without actually uttering the name.) But in his annotation of Bergmann's book Celan now replaces the four letters of the name YHWH with three simple dots.[116] 'Ye shall not profane My holy name', said the Lord, but Celan has simply un-named Him altogether. The 'sanctification' of *Ha Shem* is silence and its implied absence.

Almost every Jewish blessing begins with the phrase *Baruch atah Adonai Eloheinu*, 'Blessed art thou, O Lord our God'. In his poem 'Psalm', Celan visits the Holocaust, and becomes the earth and clay and dust to which the dead have been reduced, and out of which (as in the first moment of human Creation from dust in Genesis) the Lord 'moulds us again.' But now there is no Lord. 'No one moulds us.' Instead of 'Blessed art thou, O Lord our God' of the Hebrew blessing, we read 'Blessed art Thou, No One' (*Gelobt seist du, Niemand*).

> *No one moulds us again out of earth and clay,*
> *no one incants our dust.*
> *No one.*

---

[116] Felstiner 1995, 153.

Blessed art Thou, No One.
For your sake
we shall flower.
Towards
you.

A nothing
we were, are now, and ever shall
shall be, flowering:
the Nothing- , the
No-One's Rose.

With
our pistil soul-bright,
with our stamen heaven-ravaged,
our corolla red
from the crimson word which we sang
over, O over
the thorn.

In 'Psalm' the earthen earth-bound victims of mass murder are 'a Nothing' (*Ein Nichts*) and we have become, in Celan's voice 'No-One's rose' flowering towards No-One. Again we might recall how Eckhart sought to become nothing in order to be united with the Nothing which was God, but with this theme now transposed into a world of mass murder.

But the Nothingness of 'Psalm' is not a note of final despair. We are remoulded from the dust. And in the closing lines we, the No-One's rose, flower towards No-One with our pistil and our stamen. These reproductive organs of the plant, female and male respectively, from which the fruit comes, from which new life comes, hint at renewal or redemption, a freedom of some sort and the re-establishing of meaning.

This had been Celan's longing from the beginning. One of his early works as a young man (still called Antschel at this point) recalls the coming of the Russian army to free Czernowitz from German control. The Katyusha was a Russian rocket-launcher, also known as 'Stalin's organ' – its multiple tubes resembling a rack of organ-pipes. The rumbling approach of the liberation of his town will not free him from the struggle he must now endure for the rest of his life. 'I must wrestle with Ya'akov's angel' – note the Hebraic spelling *Ya'akov* for Jacob. In the Book of Genesis (32:26-31) Jacob wrestles all night with an angel, representing God, until eventually, maimed but triumphant, he obtains a blessing from the One who would not reveal his name. We should read Celan's subsequent poetry in this light, as his fight with the nameless No One who will bestow a blessing only after the long night of agony:

> *Stay not my love now Katyusha has started its singing!*
> *Kneel, amid old organ voices it's time now to kneel.*
> *Loud rumblings now, and must I still wrestle with Ya'akov's*
> *angel?*
> *Alone among Jewish graves, beloved, I know you are*
> *weeping.*[117]

---

[117] Felstiner 1995, 25.

REFRACTIONS.

THE BRITISH SCIENTIST Isaac Newton (1642-1727) conducted experiments with light and prisms. He showed how a single white beam of light, when shone through a prism, was bent in a different direction and divided up into several colours or wavelengths. This is because light of different wavelengths (and so different colours) was bent to different degrees. He wasn't the first to do this, of course, but he also showed that you could re-combine these multiple colours using a second prism to reconstitute the single white beam. This effect on the light by the prism is called 'refraction'.

There is, you might say, a 'single white light' running through this book: one single idea about the meaning of the word 'God', or about how Jews and Christians have used the word 'God'. We have traced it in various ways through thousands of years of belief, celebration, critical thought, prayer and suffering. In this second part of the book I am going to shine that 'single white light' onto various prisms to offer very brief 'refractions' – colourful effects caused by the shining of the light through different prisms.

These refractions are designed to be read, each one once or twice, and then pondered on – or maybe discussed with friends. I wouldn't recommend just galloping through them all in your hurry to get to the end of the book. You might view some as meditations, some as thought-experiments, some as a brief glimpse of a half-formed idea, allusive rather than descriptive, suggestive rather than conclusive.

They are not meant to be a proof of anything, but provocations to think about the difficult idea of God as Nothing in contexts that might shed light on it, and in ways which might help to free us from the 'picture' – the false picture – that our language constantly paints for us, which misleads us into thinking that God is a person.

REFRACTION 1.

TIME AND ETERNITY

IF GOD IS the Creator, if he is the answer to the question, 'Why does anything exist, rather than nothing existing?' then he cannot be 'one of the things that exist'. This view underlies the whole of what we have said so far. We can explore particular implications of this idea.

For example, an essential part of the world of things is the dimension of time. All creatures exist in a continuum of *before*, and *now*, and *after*. We all have a yesterday, a today and a tomorrow – except for a few of us who will die today, and so have no tomorrow.

That is just the condition of being a person – or an animal or plant or a stone for that matter. We exist in time. It is a fundamental dimension of our existence. It is the reality all beings: they come into being, they exist and they are destroyed *in time*. Things are capable of change, and change only exists in time, because every change implies a *before* and an *after*.

Time is therefore a fundamental part of the world, but it is only possible to think of time *within* that created world. The idea of time outwith the order of existing things, their movement and change, makes no sense at all. But if God is the Creator of all that exists, and therefore not part of creation, he must therefore also be outside that continuum of time. God cannot be 'in time'.

This is the meaning of the word 'eternity'. It doesn't mean, 'going on and on endlessly', 'an infinite length of time', because an infinite length of time is still time. 'Eternity' means 'being outside of time altogether'.

And because God is outside time, with no before and no after, God must also be beyond all change. Because change happens only in time, in the sequential ordering of events.

If God is beyond all time and beyond change, then all kinds of things follow. In spite of lots of things that believers often say about God, he cannot:

- be affected by events in time
- change his mind
- remain the same – for that would also require him to be in time
- learn anything by 'seeing' or 'hearing' what is going on in his creation.

Of course the *images* people use in prayer, preaching, theology, and so on sometimes appear to treat God as a someone, a being in time, someone with a before, a now and after. But we must remember that these are only pictures. They are not accurate descriptions of God. They are not descriptions of God at all. Nothing is or can be a description of God.

REFRACTION 2.

WHEN WE PRAY

IN OUR LAST 'Refraction' I spoke about God as being completely outside time (eternal) and therefore beyond all change. This seems to raise problems with some aspects of Christian life and ways of talking. For example, what happens when we pray?

Prayer comes in all shapes and sizes. People praise God for his glory. We thank God for her gifts to us. And we *ask* God for things: 'give us this day our daily bread.' We ask for food and forgiveness. And it is this asking which I take as the paradigm of prayer.

Now normally, if we are talking to another person, when we ask for something we are asking that person to respond, to change in some way.

If I ask my aunt for a bottle of whisky, I want my aunt to change. I want her to start thinking a certain kind of thought, get out of her chair, go to the cupboard and bring out the bottle of *Caol Ila* that she put there last week.

So what happens when I pray? According to the *grammar* of prayer – 'I ask you (God) to do this' – there are two individuals: me and God. And I am asking God to do something, to change in some way in response to my prayer. That is the picture implicit in the grammar. But if God is the Eternal Creator, outside time, how can he change?

We need to avoid being bewitched by the picture. If God

is the creator, then he creates everything that is and everything that happens. That means he creates me, he creates my desire for whisky, he *creates my prayer*, he creates the whisky, and he may (or may not) create my aunt's decision to provide me with the bottle. This God, outside time, beyond change, creates that entire process – the desire, the asking, the reply – all at once, eternally, without undergoing any change.

The *picture* of 'A asking B for something' is just that: a picture we employ. The prayer is a kind of dance or poem of faith that we perform. Not because we think that God will change his mind and do what we want, but because by that dance we perform who we are in relation to God. By creating that dance in us, by creating our prayer, God recreates us.

Perhaps we can remind ourselves of Paul's description of prayer (Galatians 4:6): 'Now because you are his children, God has sent the Spirit of his Son into our hearts to cry out, "Abba! Father!"' Our prayer is God's spirit crying out within us. If it exists, God created it. That is true of our prayer as well. When we pray, God creates us, our prayer, and the answer to our prayer, in his one eternal act.

REFRACTION 3.

FORGIVE US OUR TRESPASSES

ANOTHER THING PEOPLE often do is to ask God for forgiveness. They recognise their failure to live up to the vision and ideals that they believe in and strive after. So they pray: 'Forgive us our trespasses.'

Again let us consider the picture that is at play here. Imagine I have a friend, and we get on very well together for years, but one day I say something very offensive. My friend is hurt, and turns away from me. I ask her to forgive me, and eventually she does. She lets go of her anger and distress, and we are reconciled and return to a full friendship – perhaps even a fuller friendship with a new depth of mutual understanding.

But that picture only works as a literal description when we are talking about two individuals, two separate and distinct persons, who exist together in time. It implies the ability to change: my offensive words change my friend's mind from happiness to pain; my apology causes another change, helping her to return to peace and friendship. But God is not another individual alongside me, and God is not in time and so has no before and after, and so cannot be hurt, and cannot change his mind. If 'forgiveness' implies a change in someone's mind, God cannot literally 'forgive' me.

Returning to that core insight that God is the Creator of

all that is and all that happens, we might say something like this. When I fail to love and act as I should, it is I myself who am hurt – not God. My 'relationship' with God is damaged, we might say, because I have damaged myself. God has not changed. I have not 'made God angry', for God is unchanging and remains 'faithful', even when we are unfaithful. It is not God but I who have changed.

And then I may change again, when I ask God to forgive me; but if I do it is simply because God the Creator has already 'created a new heart in me' (Psalm 51:10). It is God's faithfulness to me that has turned me towards him. He never turned away, but I did, and it is his 'forgiveness' that has turned me back. I am only able to ask for 'forgiveness' because God has *already* done it, has created in me my longing for healing.

Of course, being human, we use pictures to express our experience. We see hurt and forgiveness in the world around us every day, and we use this picture to say something about our life in God. But when we use this imagery about God, we do so in a very different way. The imagery is not a literal representation of reality, because there is no such thing as a literal representation of God.

One rather encouraging aspect of this view is this: we never need to worry about whether we can be forgiven. Because as soon as you feel sorry, as soon as you seek forgiveness, you know that it is because you have *already* been forgiven. The forgiveness is the cause of your sorrow, not something you have to earn or wait for. It has already happened.

REFRACTION 4.

WITTGENSTEIN LOOKS AT THE WORLD

ONE OF THE thinkers who has helped to shape the single thought of this book has been Ludwig Wittgenstein. One reason for this is that he shares with me, Thomas Aquinas and the long orthodox Christian tradition, this view of the question of 'God':

> It is not *how* things are in the world that is mystical, but *that* it exists. To view the world sub specie aeterni is to view it as a whole – a limited whole. Feeling the world as a limited whole – it is this that is mystical. (1961, 73)

Wittgenstein would come back to this theme many years later, even though much else of his philosophical outlook had changed:

> If someone who believes in God looks around and asks, "Where does everything I see come from? Where does all this come from?" he is *not* craving for a (causal) explanation ... He is expressing an attitude to *all* explanations. But how is this manifested in his life? ... the believer's "God made

it" is certainly not *explanatory* – not if an explanation is supposed to have predictive power or to be less puzzling than its *explanandum*' (1980, 85).

The language of 'God' begins when we treat the world, everything that exists, as a given, and when we use language to ask a question about it as a whole. Of course the language is only a series of pictures that we have learned to play with: we say 'he' and we treat the word 'God' grammatically as if it were someone's name, and he lives in 'heaven' which sounds like a place. These are pictures we use to express what Wittgenstein calls the 'mystical', or what Aquinas calls *incognitum* 'the unknown'. We are like the poet in Shakespeare's *A Midsummer Night's Dream*:

> *The poet's eye, in fine frenzy rolling,*
> *Doth glance from heaven to Earth, from Earth to heaven.*
> *And as imagination bodies forth*
> *The forms of things unknown, the poet's pen*
> *Turns them to shapes and gives to airy nothing*
> *A local habitation and a name.*

I like the idea of theology as a 'fine frenzy'. We compose 'names and shapes' to talk about an 'airy nothing'. It is meaningless to say that these pictures are 'objectively true' or 'objectively false', because they do not refer to an object. Their 'truth' or 'falsity' do not depend on their corresponding to some object (there is no such object); their meaning is their role in the game of life which we call 'belief' or 'faith'.

To look for something called 'God' among the things that exist is therefore to misunderstand the way that language is being used. Even if you found some being, it would not be what the believer is talking about. Your failure to find such a being is, according to the believer, a foregone conclusion.

REFRACTION 5.

WITTGENSTEIN IS NOT LOOKING FOR AN ARGUMENT

AS WE HAVE seen, to ask about the 'truth' of religious language cannot mean trying to discover something 'in heaven' or anywhere else that corresponds to our pictures. For Wittgenstein, to understand religious language you don't look up to heaven. You look at the way the language is used in a human community, the way of life that it invokes, the games that people play with it, the way that pictures are used.

If someone said: 'Wittgenstein, do you believe in this?' I'd say: 'No.' 'Do you contradict the man?' I'd say: 'No.' ... Suppose someone is ill and he says: 'This is a punishment,' and I say: 'If I'm ill, I don't think of punishment at all.' If you say: 'Do you believe the opposite?' – you can call it believing the opposite, but it is entirely different from what we would normally call believing the opposite. I think differently, in a different way. I say different things to myself. I have different pictures. It is this way: if someone said: 'Wittgenstein, you don't take illness as punishment, so what do you believe?' – I'd say: 'I don't have any thoughts of punishment.' .... I give an explanation: 'I don't believe in ...', but then the religious person never believes what I describe. I can't say. I can't contradict that person. In one sense, I understand all he says – the English words 'God', 'separate', etc. I understand. I could say: 'I don't believe in this', and that would be true, meaning I haven't got these thoughts or anything that hangs together with them. But not that I could contradict the thing (1966, 53-5).

For Wittgenstein the question of belief is not about the existence of some being called 'God'. It is about whether you can find a meaning for yourself within a way of talking. You might say it's more like 'getting a joke' than accepting an argument. You either get it or you don't. You are either moved by this story to see the world in this light, or you're not.

You might want to say that this allows the word 'God' to be used simply to legitimate any community practice that it is used for. And so it would seem. 'God' actually *has* been used to support all kinds of things – the burning of witches, the exclusion of women from social positions, the slaughter of war, the acquisition of inordinate wealth.

But the critique of these uses (or abuses) of the word 'God' does not lie in some abstract notion of what God is like. It lies in the life of a community and its human history. We don't know what God is like, but we do know the story which believers tell each other in which the hand of God is 'seen' when people are freed from slavery, when prophets challenge injustice. Above all for Christians the meaning of the word 'God' is seen in Jesus ('the image of the invisible God') forgiving those who offend, healing the sick, welcoming the excluded, and in his teaching about mercy and justice – feed the hungry, clothe the naked, forgive those who hurt you. The ethical use of the word 'God' is constructed out of these historical (or pseudo-historical) narratives and the community practices that attend them.

It is as Wittgenstein says: 'For a large class of cases ... the meaning of a word is its use in the language' (1958, §43).

REFRACTION 6.

CONTEXT GIVES MEANING

I HAVE ARGUED that the word 'God' is not the name of some object to whom you can refer in prayer or in theological discussion. This is a remark about the language, the way the word is used. You can't use 'God' in a straightforward way to identify the object of your attention, using a word to direct yourself towards that object.

You can do this with a personal name. When I say 'Donald Trump', the personal name directs our attention towards a particular being about whom I may be about to express an opinion. But though 'God' usually *looks* like a personal name in the way it is used, it is not in fact. God is not 'a person' or an 'object of attention'. In the case of the word 'God', the meaning of the word is in some sense determined not by the word alone but by *what you do* when you use the word.

Let's return to the theme of Chapter Two above (pp. 50-55), where Amos declares that the God of Israel cannot be worshipped by wealthy people gorging themselves at big parties, lolling about on ivory couches, while they abandon the poor to suffering, injustice and death. It's not because they are worshipping the wrong god; it's not because they have chosen a different god from the God of Israel or are approaching God in the wrong way – singing the wrong songs for example. That would be a matter of their *intention* about God: they intended to worship the God of Israel, and they intended to do it according to proper forms. The problem is not the intended 'object' of their prayer. The problem concerns the things in their daily lives, the things that they have done: they have oppressed the poor and turned their backs on the needy.

The idea of 'God as Nothing' frees us from this trap: God is not a particular individual entity that you can attend to, or someone you can direct your mind at. You can't tell that the God you are praying to is the 'right one' from the kind of intention or the divine picture you have in your mind's eye, or the name you use, or whatever kind of emotional or intellectual engagement you feel with the divinity. You can tell that you are praying to the God of Israel when you look at your engagement *with other people.*

We are actually quite familiar with the idea that the same word can have one meaning in one circumstance and another meaning in a different circumstance. For example, when I utter the word 'you' in the presence of my son, it refers to him. When I utter the same word to my postman, it refers to someone else. The meaning of the word depends on the context in which it is uttered, the direction I am facing and who happens to be there.

We can think of the word 'God' like this. It behaves like the word 'you' in this respect. Just as the word 'you' means different things when spoken in different circumstances, so the word 'God' means different things when spoken in the context of the different practices and life-choices of the person who utters it – particularly, Amos tells us, her choices in respect of the poor and the powerless.

REFRACTION 7.

SAY THE WORD 'GOD'

WHAT ARE WE doing when we say the word 'God'?

It looks as if we are naming an individual being. That is the way the grammar seems to work. When we use the word 'God' in a sentence, it *looks* as if it is a personal name – like 'Barbara' or 'Bob'. But as I have shown in the course of this book, in the Christian tradition the word doesn't work like that.

The word 'god' comes from a Proto-Germanic word, *guthan*, which developed into *gott* in German and *god* in Old English. It absolutely did *not* mean the Creator, the one whom Jesus called 'Father'. It was a common noun, a word for a certain kind of thing.

What kind of thing was a *guthan* or a *god*? The ancient Germanic tribes entertained a whole raft of beings whom they called gods. It seems unlikely that they had 'faith' in these gods in the sense that Christians, Jews or Muslims have faith. They simply thought that such beings existed and were a part (a strange and dangerous part) of the universe in which they also lived. And because these gods liked to be respected, and because they were quite angry sometimes and could do you harm, it was a good idea to keep them happy with occasional sacrifices and libations. It was a kind of bargain: 'I'll do this for you, and you (please) do that for me.' Or as the Romans said, *do ut des,* 'I give so that you might give.' Of course the same kind of thing was true of a Greek god (*theos*) or a Roman god (*deus*).

This seems to have been the case generally with the ancient gods of Europe, whether Celtic, Germanic, Roman or Greek. They were numerous individuals, interacting with people, making demands, raping women, procreating with each other, murdering each other, choosing their favourites among humans, and laying waste whole cities together with their inhabitants. They had stories.

But as we saw in Chapter 1, when we compared the creation stories of the Babylonians with the creation story of Genesis in the Bible, a central *aim* of the Genesis story was to remove all gods from the narrative. The same is true of the borrowing of the word *guthan* or *gott* by the English-speaking Christian when he or she says 'God'. If we are going to talk about the unknown and unknowable ground of all being, we will have to use words. And all our words reflect the finite thing-ness of daily human experience, because that is what human language grew out of. That is perfectly all right as long as we remember this: using the word *god* does not mean we worship a god. Forget the etymological origin of the word. It is a word we have stolen, but for Christians and Jews it means something utterly different from what it meant to those who invented it and applied it to Woden (for example). There are no gods.

REFRACTION 8.

LOVING GOD: WHAT'S GOING ON?

WE HAVE ALREADY discussed the question of 'loving God' (pp. 74-78), and seen how the commandment to 'love God' is only intelligible in terms of loving one another, and that in the end nothing else counts as loving God. God is not a member of the list of 'lovable individuals', because he is not a member of any list (*non est in genere*) and because he is not an individual or a potential object of your love.

In this view, that we 'love God' by loving one another, we are still joined to God by love, but it is not our love for God that is at stake here. It is 'not that we loved God, but that he loved us' (1 John 4:10). It is our grateful knowledge and acceptance of *being loved* that defines what it means for us to 'love God', knowing that God's love is the cause of our existence. And knowing also that God's love is the cause of the existence of other people, and other things.

God's 'love' is not like ours. We love things because they are good. Their goodness – whatever that might be – is what gives rise to our love, drawing love out of us. But in the case of God, he is not changed by creatures, so nothing that a creature does can make God love it. It cannot possibly be that he loves us because we are good or lovable. It is not the goodness of things (or people) that makes God love them. It

217

is the fact that God loves them that makes them exist, and makes them good.

If God's love for you is the cause of your existence and the cause of your goodness, there is nothing you can do, or need to do, to earn that love. You can't love another person in order to earn the love of God. It's rather that your love of another person reveals the love of God in you. That love which unites the Father and the Son, the love which makes the Father and the Son one and equal, is known in Christian tradition as the Holy Spirit. That Holy Spirit 'poured into our hearts' is the source of the love with which we love one another. It is also the love that makes the believer, like Jesus Christ, a son or daughter, one with and equal to the Father.

REFRACTION 9.

BEWITCHED BY GRAMMAR

CHRISTIANS AND OTHER monotheists (Jews and Muslims for example) have to use ordinary human language when they talk about what they believe in. As T. S. Eliot wrote in *Sweeney Agonistes*, 'I gotta use words when I talk to you.'

The problem is that the languages we use are all designed as ways of talking about things which exist in the world. The grammar of our language reflects the structure of that world, in which there are very large numbers of interacting individuals.

Subject-verb-object: 'The fox ate the chicken.' Two nouns (with definite articles) and a verb connecting them. We have two nouns, a subject and an object, because there are two individuals involved in our observation, a fox and a chicken. These are two actually existing things in space and time, with two names. One being did something to another being. There is a fox which exists, and there is a chicken which exists (or used to exist before the fox ate it). The grammar of our sentence reflects the structure of the world of existing things.

When we talk about God we can only do so in the language or languages we know. There is no special new language with its own grammar that enables us to talk 'accurately' about God. That means we have to use the words and grammar that grew out of our talking about existing things, and so it *seems* as if when we say 'God' we are talking about an existing being, a being among other beings.

So we use the grammar of subject-verb-object when we say a sentence like 'God loves you'. But as we have seen, the word 'God' is not the name of one of the existing things that there are. It's a perfectly true sentence, but it's not true in any way that we can really understand.

God's love is the reason you exist. It is the reason anything exists, rather than nothing existing. So saying 'God loves you' is clearly not about two already existing beings, side by side, interacting with each other as a fox and a chicken interact. This is about the love that makes you exist in the first place. It is actually an account of *your* existence, a description of you, a claim that the reason you exist is that you are loved. What *seems* to tell us something about God's 'state of mind' (warm feelings towards you) actually does nothing of the sort. It actually tells us about you, and speaks about the mystery of your existence.

REFRACTION 10.

BEWITCHED BY PRONOUNS

IT HAS BECOME conventional in most contexts to use masculine pronouns when talking about God. We say, 'He created the world', and 'His mercy endures for ever.' Of course, it is completely legitimate to use feminine pronouns too – 'She hears the cry of the poor' would be perfectly acceptable. And the Bible has plenty of feminine images of God – a woman who hunts for a coin she has lost (Luke 15:8), a mother who breast-feeds and comforts her child (Isaiah 66:12-13), or a mother-hen gathering her chicks under her wings (Luke 13:34).

But our use of masculine or feminine pronouns, or our use of masculine and feminine images, suggest absolutely nothing about the 'gender of God'. It is meaningless to talk of the gender or sex of God, but it is worth wondering what our use of gendered language implies.

For example, does the use of masculine imagery for God imply that men are more godlike than women? Does it justify the organisation of male power in society? That was certainly what the American theologian Mary Daly thought was implied by such male pronouns. She wrote, 'If God is male, then the male is God'.

No doubt male-pronoun God-talk *can* be used in that way. But there are other ways of understanding it. Let us try to imagine what else male-pronoun God-talk might mean. Remember that using *images* to talk about God does not tell us what God is like, but rather tells us about ourselves in relation to God. To call God 'Father'. for example, implies that we are all 'children of God', and therefore we are all sisters and brothers. And if we are all sisters and brothers we belong to each other, and are called to love one another.

When God is called 'Father' in relation to us, it tells us something else about humanity. For the image of fatherhood in the Bible is not only about God's 'fatherly care' for Israel and for humanity. It also speaks of generativity. This is a metaphor drawn from the world of sexuality and reproduction. A father is one who has generated a child. As God is shown in the Gospel as the divine father of Jesus, so Mary is shown as his human mother:

> 'The Holy Spirit will come upon you,
> and the power of the Most High will overshadow you;
> therefore the child to be born will be called holy,
> the Son of God' (Luke 1:35).

And humanity discovers what Mary discovered: to respond to God is to be receptive to the Spirit, to bear fruit, to give flesh to God's word in the world. The language is gendered, certainly. But the picture of God as Father in this account makes all humanity – women *and* men – 'female' in this respect. Mary's receptiveness is the paradigm for all Christians. To be a Christian, in the context of this gendered imagery at least, is to become 'a woman', to bring to birth the Word made flesh.

REFRACTION 11.

MY GOD, YOUR GOD

IN 2015 DR Layricia Hawkins was teaching political science at an Evangelical Protestant college in Illinois, Wheaton College. She was much concerned with the relationship between Christianity and Islam, energised by solidarity with Muslims who were increasingly the target of public hostility and suspicion. She donned a hijab – a characteristically (though not exclusively) Islamic head-covering for women – as a statement of solidarity with her Muslim sisters. This caused a flurry of comment. But what got her into trouble was her claim that Christians and Muslims worship 'the same God'.

In short order she was placed on administrative leave by the college authorities. She was not cowed, however, and quoted the pope among others in support of her position: 'As Pope Francis stated last week, we worship the same God.' Citing the pope in your support might help in some circles, but many American evangelicals regard him as the anti-Christ, so it's not guaranteed to work.

The events led to a public controversy about whether it was true, or acceptable, to say that Christians and Muslims worship the 'same God'.

Some stated that Christians believe that God is a Trinity and Muslims don't, so they couldn't believe in the same God. But of course Jews don't seem to believe God is a Trinity either, but few would doubt that the God worshipped by Jews (whom

Jesus called 'Father') was the 'same God' as Christians worship.

What was missing from much of the debate, however, was any question of what exactly the expression 'the same God' might mean.

You might think it pretty straightforward. If I say, 'My mother is the same as the head of this crime-gang', there are objective conditions *in the world* which would establish this as true or false. This is possible because 'my mother' and 'gang boss' are both references to an individual being or beings in the world.

But 'God' is not the name of an individual being. When Christians and Muslims say 'God' they mean a lot of things, but at the heart of their meanings is this: that they think the world is created. They look at everything that exists and recognise that its existence constitutes a mystery, and they call that mystery 'God'. *In that sense* we can say that they worship 'the same God': not because they refer to the same individual, but because they refer to the same experience of the mystery of the world.

As Christians and Muslims have explored that mystery, as individuals and communities shaped by their experiences, many have come to quite different conclusions about what it means, and what it implies for their lives.

For some the differences might be about the Trinity, about Christ as the Incarnate Word, about the *Umma* versus the Church, about law versus grace. But for others the 'identity' of God might be more closely related to what is *done* 'in the name of God'. I might then ask myself, as a Catholic Christian, whether I worship 'the same God' as the *Conquistadores* who raped and plundered their way around South America. As a Sunni Muslim I might ask myself whether I worship 'the same God' as the ISIS fighters who murdered, captured, raped and sold Yazidi women. Do I worship 'the same God' as someone (Christian, Jewish or Muslim) who feeds the hungry in the name of God?

The very notion of 'the same God' is so fraught with grammatical and moral problems, that the question itself seems to implode, becoming unintelligible.

REFRACTION 12.

THE FOOL SPEAKS IN HIS HEART

AS WE SAW in Chapter 7, when Thomas Aquinas wonders whether the existence of God is 'self-evident' (*per se notum*), he answers 'no, it can't be', because in Psalm 14 we read of someone who doesn't believe in God: 'The fool has said in his heart, "There is no God"' (*Dixit insipiens in corde suo, non est Deus*). Clearly the existence of God is not self-evident, as this fool denies it.

But there is nothing else in the entire psalm about God or his existence. The whole thing is a discussion of wickedness, and in particular the oppression of the poor.

They are corrupt, they do abominable deeds,
there is none that does any good.
The Lord looks down from heaven
*   upon the children of men,*
to see if there are any that act wisely,
that seek after God.
They have all gone astray, they are
*   all alike corrupt;*
there is not one that does good,
no, not one.
Have they no knowledge, all the evildoers

who eat up my people as though they ate bread,
and do not call upon the Lord?
There they shall be in great terror,
for God is with the generation of the righteous.
You would confound the plans of the poor,
but the Lord is his refuge.

O that deliverance for Israel would come out of Zion!
When the Lord restores the fortunes of his people,
Jacob shall rejoice, Israel shall be glad.

The question of God in this psalm is not a philosophical one, about some being which might or might not exist. It is a moral one.

REFRACTION 13.

HOW WILL WE RECOGNISE HIS PRESENCE

IF GOD IS no thing, what does it mean to say, as believers sometimes do, 'He is present'? Or for that matter, what would it mean to say he is 'absent'?

Of course for a believer, he is always present, in creative power. It is God's 'presence' to what exists that is the cause of its existence. He is closer to me than I am to myself (I have cited this sentence from Augustine before).

But Christians talk about 'presence' in other ways too, in additional ways. And this is not a question of 'someone' being there in addition to 'anyone else' who was there.

If I throw a party and invite five people and they all come, but one of them brings a friend, then there will be an extra person 'present' – I'm sure we'll manage. I'll lay another place, and there will be seven at the table.

But if I invite five people to a party and all six of us start to pray (well, it might happen), we might then say God was present. (And of course, we should remember that he is present whether we pray or not.) But that doesn't mean that there are seven people at the party – or seven of *anything*. There are still six. God is 'One', but he is not 'one more at the party', even though he is 'present'.

We say God is present when:

- we feed the hungry and clothe the naked (Matthew 25).
- two or three are gathered in Christ's name (Matthew 18:20).
- we share bread and wine in memory of Christ's death and resurrection (Luke 24).
- when someone's heart is broken ('The Lord is close to the broken-hearted', Psalm 34:18).

But this kind of language is not meant to describe the presence of some 'being', which might otherwise have been absent. It isn't like an invisible person (a ghost or spirit, for example) who might have just turned up. The way believers talk about the 'presence of God' without seeking to identify an individual who has become present, who has 'turned up', shows that in fact we don't think that God is an individual at all.

REFRACTION 14.

IMAGES OF GOD

MANY PEOPLE WILL no doubt object to our account of God as Nothing. They will say, 'But look at what Christians say. They constantly talk about God, or talk *to* God, as if he were a person, a great invisible and omnipresent individual. You can't just ignore the way Christians actually talk.'

But Christians know perfectly well, if they think about such things, that the language they use about God is used in strange ways, being forced to mean things which are beyond its scope. They see, for example, the way that God is described in the Bible in countless different images, but they don't take these as literal descriptions of God.

Sometimes these words are metaphors. In the Hebrew Bible we learn that:

- God has wings (Ps. 91:4; 57:1)
- God can forget or need reminding or waking up (Genesis 8:1; Ps. 106.4; 44:23).
- God has fingers (Ps. 8:3)
- God is a rock and a fortress (Psalm 18:2)
- God is a sun (*shemesh*) and a shield (Psalm 84:11)
- God wears shoes (Psalm 108:9)
- God is a moth (Hosea 5:12).

But it would be absurd to think that Christians and Jews

worship a winged entity, an actual rock, or a moth. If Christians and Jews don't take these literally, we may suspect that other aspects of the grammar of 'God' (i.e. the ways we use the word 'God') are not what they seem.

In fact you could say that 'being a Christian' includes among other things a life-long process of learning how to speak (or write, or read) about God without knowing what we are talking about. It is a process in which we use images of God, while at the same time learning that they do not give us information about God. It is a process, you might say, of watching our language collapse in the face of the unspeakable.

These metaphors – fire, moth, rock etc. – are actually hugely important because, among other things, they teach us to speak about God while at the same time understanding perfectly well that these words don't give us information about God. The words play a role in our lives, but the role they play is not that of 'representing God'. We are not likely to make the mistake of worshipping a fuzzy insect because God has said he is a moth.

Language about God is stretched to breaking point, and beyond.

REFRACTION 15.

LOOKING FOR GOD IN THE EAST

IN THE FIRST centuries of Christianity, there was something very important about looking east. When someone was baptised they first looked to the west to 'renounce the devil', to reject evil, and then they turned to the east to accept Christ, to say the prayer that Jesus had taught his disciples (the 'Our Father'). Why should points of the compass be given theological meaning in this way?

The simple answer is that the sun rises in the east. The prophet had written, 'The Sun will rise with healing in his wings' (Malachi 4:2), and that image was applied to Christ. Christ was therefore 'the Sun'. Later he would be addressed in song as *Sol Iustitiae* 'the Sun of Justice'. So to attend to Christ the Sun, to await the justice of God's rising kingdom, you faced east.

Likewise, the Irish monk Columbanus (d. 615) expected his fellow-monks to stand still and face east when they made the Sign of the Cross – a gesture of wordless prayer over their bodies and faces – except when they were in a hurry. And for the same reason, for most of the Church's history church buildings, with very few exceptions, were constructed facing east, so that the priest and the whole congregation would all be facing east during the celebration of their liturgy. Because

Paradise is in the east, and the sun rises in the east, and Christ is in the east, and Christ will come from the east at the end of time – 'For as lightning that comes from the east is visible even in the west, so will be the coming of the Son of Man' (Matthew 24:27). God is in the east. In the late-second century Tertullian noted that his contemporaries thought Christians worshipped the sun, because they met on *Dies Solis* ('Sun-day') and prayed facing east.

But of course, Christians do not worship the sun – that great inferno of nuclear fusion. They use the sun as a picture to point to what is unimaginable. They do not face east because they think that Christ or God is *actually* in the east. If anything they believe that God and Christ are 'everywhere' – or 'in heaven' which is 'nowhere'. Just imagine if you longed to call on God in prayer but didn't know which way was east? Would it matter that you didn't know? Might you accidentally 'pray to the devil' by facing west? The thought is absurd.

Facing east is a dance, a drama, an act of poetic appropriation of a natural image – the warming, life-giving, illuminating sun – to help believers to speak of what is unspeakable.

When people observe Christians talking about 'God' using nouns, verbs and adjectives that are appropriate to various individual beings, it is easy to see why they make the mistake of thinking that Christians believe in an individual being called 'God'. They are using language that usually refers to individual beings, and the grammar of theology and prayer seems to point in that direction.

But we should understand those ways of talking in the same way we understand the dance of 'facing east'. Of course, facing east is serious: it is a powerful image of waiting in expectation, of 'orientation' to God you might say. But no matter what it looks like, it does not express a belief that God is actually in the east.

Likewise, the Christian language of God in theology

and prayer, no matter what it *looks like*, is not a language about some powerful invisible being in addition to all the other beings, visible or invisible, that there might be. If you are tempted to take the language literally, and imagine an individual being called 'God', you should go outside, face east, and ask yourself if you, or anyone else, thinks that God is 'over in that direction'.

REFRACTION 16.

SCIENTIFIC 'NEW ATHEISM'

I HAVE AVOIDED discussing the 'New Atheists' (or even the older atheists) so far. This book is not meant to be an answer to their arguments; it is an exploration of a view of God which effectively makes their arguments irrelevant, just as it makes the fundamentalist views of some religious people irrelevant. But it is worth touching on the issue briefly.

If God is the Creator of all that exists, then God cannot be part of the world of interconnected beings which act upon each other and are the subject of scientific enquiry, which is the empirical, experimental, methodical approach to things that exist. Science investigates phenomena; but God is not any kind of phenomenon, and no phenomenon that any scientist could ever discover could possibly be God.

So we read Alain de Botton: 'I recall my father reducing my sister to tears in an attempt to dislodge her modestly held notion that a reclusive god might dwell somewhere in the universe' (2012, 13). But we remind ourselves that for believers there are no gods dwelling anywhere in the universe.

Christopher Hitchens urges: 'Thanks to the telescope and the microscope, [religion] no longer offers an explanation for anything important' (2007, 282). Of course, he is absolutely right. Religion (and by implication God) are not explanations of anything – unless understood in a completely non-scientific way as an 'explanation' of *everything* (which is not actually an explanation at all). Nothing that is discovered by a telescope or a microscope could ever be God, or be evidence of God.

Richard Dawkins writes that 'the existence of God is a scientific hypothesis like any other. Even if hard to test in practice ... God's existence or non-existence is a scientific fact about the universe' (2006, 24). So he treats the question of God as if it were about the discoverability of some particular being which must be vastly complicated in order to have created such a complex universe (184-9). Again, whatever Dawkins is looking for – or trying to disprove – it has nothing to do with the God envisioned by Christian belief.

These New Atheists are absolutely right to reject any god conceived in such a 'scientist' way. But they are simply repeating the rejection of the gods by the author of Genesis, by Augustine, Aquinas and Eckhart. Believers have no interest in any god which can be discovered by scientific enquiry. Anything which can be demonstrated by science is *ipso facto* not God, and Christians may not worship it on pain of idolatry.

It is as if atheists like Dawkins and Hitchens have just gone to church and heard their first sermon, where the preacher quite properly told them that there are no gods. And then they have run away. The position they have come to, which they imagine is a critique of Christianity, is actually the *starting point* of Christian theology. They have merely swept away the idolatries.

REFRACTION 17.

THE THEOLOGY OF ONE LETTER

THEOLOGY OR 'GOD-TALK' comes in many different shapes and sizes. It might be philosophical reflection on 'what exists' and why. It might be textual interpretation, thinking about what a text might mean in all its multi-layerdness, and what does it mean anyway to say a text 'means something'? It might involve thinking about the moral demands that faith makes – how we deal with our enemies, or climate change, or our ageing parents.

All these things are actually ways of thinking about the world, that is to say about creation, about everything that exists. They are all *ways of reading* the world with reference to God. Sometimes this might seem a little strange. Someone might experience their suffering as 'punishment', for example, though God cannot literally punish anyone as we have seen (this would require him to respond to a human action).

But feeling 'punished' is a way of reading the world as significant. It cannot be either right or wrong about 'the facts of the matter', because it isn't about facts. It is rather the kind of playful or dramatic creativity which makes every person an artist or a poet – looking for meaning, or creating meaning out of experience.

Speaking of such creative playfulness, I have always

enjoyed the rabbinic interpretation of Genesis, the first book of the Bible. Or more specifically, the interpretation of the first letter of the first word of the Bible. It begins *Bereshit bara' Elohim*:

$$\text{בְּרֵאשִׁית בָּרָא אֱלֹהִים}$$

That is: 'In the beginning, God created ....' Now, remember that Hebrew reads from right to left ('backwards' as my children say, being a bit ethnocentric). So the first letter is on the right-hand side. It is called *bet* in Hebrew and is pronounced /b/. Look at the shape of it: it is like a bracket.

This letter became significant in early rabbinic theology – so significant that in some scribal traditions it was greatly enlarged to make its statement. As a preposition this letter *bet* just means 'in', but its actual shape (and perhaps its size) was treated as a divine declaration by the Jerusalem Talmud, as Rabbi Jonah said: 'Just as the letter *bet* is closed on all sides and open only in front, so you are not permitted to enquire What is beneath? What is above? What came before? What will come after?' This 'bracket' encloses not only the whole Torah as a text, but stands symbolically for the enclosure of the whole of creation. Everything which exists is contained 'in front' of it – that is, to the left. Apart from that there is nothing, the divine mystery about which we are not permitted to enquire. Or perhaps 'not permitted' is not quite right. It is simply impossible to enquire, for who can enquire about Nothing, and what kind of answer could we expect of such an enquiry?

REFRACTION 18.

THE UNCAUSED CAUSE

IN CHAPTER SEVEN we considered Thomas Aquinas's 'proofs' of the existence of God, and considered that they might not be functioning as an argument against atheism, but doing something else – perhaps showing that the world raises a question, perhaps making sure that we never made the mistake of treating God as some existing being. We look at the world – everything that exists – and respond to it with puzzlement, or awe.

The 'proofs' are discussed – very briefly – in the *Summa Theologiae* (1a, 2, a.3) under the title *Utrum Deus sit* – which we might translate 'whether God is' or 'whether there is God'.

Thomas argues that in the world of 'efficient causes' (things that bring other things about) nothing can be the cause of itself. A cause always exists before the effect that it brings about, but nothing can pre-exist itself. He says in all chains of cause and effect the first cause brings about the middle one (or middle ones) and that brings about the last one. But if you take away the first cause, all the other elements in the chain will also cease to exist. And there cannot be an infinite regress of cause and effect, because an infinite regress would have no first cause, and if there were no first cause there would be no infinite chain either. Therefore there must be some first efficient cause 'which all people call God'.

Elegant though it may seem to some, few people are convinced by it as a proof of something called 'God'. In fact, even within Thomas's own terms, the argument appears to be flawed. Elsewhere he writes *Deus non est in genere*: 'God is not in any *genus* or category', i.e. not a member of any class of things (1a, 5, a.5). He cannot, therefore, be counted among the *genus* or category of causes. He can't be one cause among many, not even the first of them. He can't be a member of *any* category.

There is another way of expressing this. When A causes B, it is because they share some common space. They exist in a shared medium, within which causality is possible. Causality is simply part of the order of creation, and is only possible *within* that order. But if God is the Creator and not part of that order, then he cannot, as a matter of logic, be a cause. He is the reason for the existence of the world of time and space within which causes are possible. But he cannot be the first cause in a long series of causes, because that would make him part of that world.

It seems that Thomas's own view of causality rules out any notion that God is the first in a series of causes. Whatever this 'proof' means, then, it can't mean that. It is pointing, once again, towards the incomprehensible notion of creation. The word 'God' is simply the word we use to express the mystery of why there should be a world in which causation takes place rather than nothing at all. That mystery cannot be a 'cause' among other causes. We may use the *picture* of causation, but (like the pronoun 'he') we know it is only a picture.

REFRACTION 20.

JESUS AND THE EXISTENCE OF GOD

IT IS WORTH remembering, especially for Christians for whom Jesus is *the* defining figure, that Jesus did not proclaim the existence of God.

It hardly needed proclaiming in fact, since 'God' was already part of virtually everyone's vocabulary, part of their way of seeing and talking about the world. If Jesus had said, 'God exists' to anyone, they would have wondered what on earth he was talking about.

What Jesus proclaimed, over and over again, was the *kingdom* of God. In the original Greek of the New Testament we find the word *basileia* 'kingdom', but Jesus speaking to his Jewish contemporaries might have used the Aramaic word *malkut* (cf. Hebrew *malchut*). This word has more of a dynamic sense than 'kingdom' (which can mean simply a place or territory). *Malkut* means something more like 'rule, ruling', connected to the Hebrew word *malach* 'to rule'. So Jesus proclaimed to his hearers that this kingdom or 'ruling' of God had suddenly come among them. It was 'now', it was 'at hand' and 'among you'.

Of course God cannot have *begun* to rule. God as the Creator cannot 'begin' to do anything, as he is outside time and cannot change. 'Beginning' anything is only possible for creatures in time. What begins when the 'ruling of God' begins is that humanity, for the first time ever, does God's will. In the person of Jesus, a human being in history carries out the will of God fully, freely, whole-heartedly and generously. It is in this sense that the ruling of God breaks into history, is 'at hand' or 'among you' – not by God beginning to do something, but by humanity doing it. Jesus himself is the beginning or inbreaking of the kingdom of God.

To respond to Jesus is therefore not to assert the existence of some being called God, which Jesus had no interest in asserting. It is to recognise the presence of God in the speech and activity of Jesus, and to recognise that this human life is also a *divine* life, and that it is a life that we are all summoned to share. The Spirit that filled Christ, God-made-man, is the same Spirit that is poured out on humanity to make all human lives divine.

REFRACTION 21.

REWARD AND PUNISHMENT

IN SOME CHRISTIAN writings we find descriptions of reward and punishment. There is a picture: if you behave in this way, you will be rewarded (eternal life, a heavenly banquet, the bosom of Abraham, a garden of delights). If you behave in a different way, you will be punished (fire, tortures, darkness with wailing and gnashing of teeth).

As with all such language, we must remember that this is only a picture. It is a picture derived from human experience, where authority-figures (kings, law-makers, judges, etc.) attempt to create a certain public order, and do so by rewarding obedience and punishing disobedience. As a picture, it has its uses, but like much of our picturing of God it is capable of being misused and misunderstood. Wittgenstein remarked once, as recollected by his friend and student Rush Rhees: 'If I thought of God as another being like myself, outside myself, only infinitely more powerful, then I would regard it as my duty to defy him.' That would certainly apply to any God conceived of as a judge with the power to reward and punish.

Of course, God the Creator cannot literally reward and punish in the sense that this picture suggests. To reward someone is to react positively to what she does; to punish someone is to react negatively to what she does. But God cannot react to anything. A human being can react because she lives in time, is subject to change, and is influenced by the goings-on around her. None of that is true of God. So God cannot reward or punish.

There is, however, a sense in which we can talk of punishment in connection with God. Christians hold that God was made present in history in the person of Jesus, the fulness of God's love in a human life. And God-in-Christ was punished by violent men. The punishment of God is not punishment imposed by God on wicked people, but the punishment suffered by a loving God: flogging, nails, thorns, and death.

And in any case Jesus himself undermines the language of reward and punishment. 'I do not call you servants,' he says in John's Gospel. 'I call you friends.' We are not joined to God by obedience to a master who has the power to reward and punish; we are joined by love, as friends, and if friends as equals.

It may be legitimate to use the picture of reward and punishment for some purposes, rhetorical or otherwise. But to believe in Christ is in the end to be freed from the picture of divine reward and punishment altogether, and to enter into the life of God.

REFRACTION 22.

WHERE IS THE IMAGE OF GOD?

WE HAVE SEEN how the God of Israel is beyond imagination, even if we constantly use images. We have seen that all mental images of God must be broken: *Not this, not this.* But there are also times when we are told that there *is* an image of God. We read in the book of Genesis about God creating humanity: 'God created man in his own image, in the image of God he created him; male and female he created them' (1:27). We should note that the word for 'image' here is *eikon* in the Greek version of Genesis which was in use among Jews at the time of Christ.

This idea of the image of God is what shapes our reading of Matthew's Gospel, where the Pharisees ask a question of Jesus in an attempt to ensnare him (22:17-21).

> 'Tell us, then, what you think. Is it lawful to pay taxes to Caesar or not?'
>
> But Jesus, aware of their malice, said, 'Why put me to the test, you hypocrites? Show me the money for the tax.' And they brought him a coin. And Jesus said, 'Whose image and inscription is this?'
>
> They said, 'Caesar's.'
>
> Then he said to them, 'Render therefore to Caesar the

things that are Caesar's, and to God the things that are God's.'

Now this is absolutely not a division of 'religious things' from 'political things', as some commentators have suggested, where God ends up with prayer and worship and devout feelings, while Caesar gets the money and the political power. We have to see the structure of the argument Jesus is making. 'Whose image (*eikon*) is this?' You pay taxes to Caesar, the coins, because they bear the image of Caesar. What belongs to Caesar? The things that bear Caesar's image.

The implicit second stage of the argument is this, therefore: What belongs to God? In this context the answer can only be 'The things that bear God's image.' The only place where we are permitted to see God's image is in a human being, made by God in God's own image. If coins bearing Caesar's image belong to Caesar, that which bears God's image belongs to God.

It is hard to imagine how you could possibly 'render' human beings to God. (Human sacrifice, anyone?) But it is very easy to see how human beings are rendered every day to 'Caesar', to the powers of this world: to 'market forces', or 'military necessity', the state, the brutal exigencies of power and its maintenance, our pleasure or profit when we seek to use or exploit others, the sacred national borders whose preservation requires that migrants drown in the Mediterranean or lose their children in detention camps because our borders are more important than their lives. In all these instances God's image (human beings) is being rendered unto Caesar.

To 'render unto God what is God's' means to place human beings at the centre of our world, and to render them to no-one and nothing. When we recognise that people may be sacrificed to absolutely nothing, then we will have fulfilled the command to render them to God.

REFRACTION 23.

THE SUN
IS SETTING

I'D LIKE TO think a bit more about the pictures our language paints for us – the pictures we sometimes have to escape from.

I am standing in the window, looking west over the hills, and turn to my friend and say, 'The sun is setting.' He replies, 'What do you mean? The sun isn't doing anything. The world is turning and so we are losing sight of the sun. The sun is remaining absolutely motionless. Haven't you ever heard of Copernicus or Galileo?'

One of the problems that we have with talking about God is like this. When we say the sun is setting, we *look* as if we have given an account of the sun's activity, a description of the sun. In fact we have done nothing of the sort.

When we say, 'God is the Creator', we *look* as if we have given some account of God. Ah ha! so that is what he is like! But we have not. We have indicated that the world is *created*, but it does not give us information about God. We remind ourselves of Thomas Aquinas: 'we are joined to God as to the unknown.'

Logically, of course, we can say 'God is the Creator', but this does not imply anything about God as he is *per se*. If I sit opposite you at a table, talking to you, you are in front of me. If I suddenly turn round and face in the opposite direction, you are behind me. What can be said about you *logically* has changed: you were in front of me, now you are behind me. But you have not changed at all.

This analogy might help us to understand the way our language about God works. The pictures we use in God-talk express truths about the world, about ourselves, in relation to God. We really are creatures. But in respect of God, this kind of talk expresses only a 'logical relation', a feature of our grammar. So Aquinas says:

> Since God is completely outside the order of creation, and all creatures are ordered to him, but not the other way round, it is clear that creatures are really related to God himself; but in God there is no real relationship to creatures, but only according to our thought (*secundum rationem tantum*) in as much as creatures are *spoken* about in relation to him (*ST* 1a, 13, 7).

What *looks* like language about God, what *looks* like an account of God, is a trick of our language. If I say, 'I baked this cake', it establishes a relationship between two things. It says something about me, and it says something about the cake. I really am a baker; this cake really is baked.

But though the same *picture* appears in our minds when we say, 'God created the world', Aquinas denies the equivalence. Being a cake-baker is a fact about what I am like, describing a real feature of my life. Being the Creator is not a fact about what God is like. It is merely the logical implication of describing the world as created.

REFRACTION 24.

DECONSTRUCTING WITH DERRIDA

I WILL CLOSE this series of short refractions, and close the entire book, with a slightly longer one in honour of the Algerian-born French philosopher Jacques Derrida (1930-2004). Some of his fellow-philosophers admired him, while others held him in furious disdain. I am still not quite sure where I stand myself within that spectrum, but I find in one of his late works, *Circumfession*, a powerful expression of the kind of theology that I am seeking to articulate.

Derrida's thought is most familiar to us through his notion of *deconstruction*. He himself was reluctant to define this term – partly because the whole point of deconstruction was to resist the definable, to resist the idea that words had fixed and clear meanings. Deconstruction was itself the process of the endless dismantling of the apparent meanings of language (and of laws, institutions, arts, etc.), questioning the assumptions of every statement, exposing the *aporias* or self-contradictions in a text, by which the text unravelled its own meaning. He argued (or perhaps 'demonstrated') that text existed and had meaning not in relation to some reality it referred to but in the context of a whole universe of other texts. For Derrida language and its signs related not directly to some objective world 'out there', but simply to other signs.

Part of this deconstruction was to show how a text (or other set of signs) reflected the structures of power in society, how it embodied and reinforced that power, how it marginalized dissent and so on. The task of deconstruction is to unmask the power embedded in language and, in exposing its hidden workings, to reduce its power over us. The task of deconstruction is 'constantly to suspect, to criticize the given determinations of culture, of institutions, of legal systems, not in order to destroy them or simply to cancel them, but to be just with justice, to respect this relation to the other as justice.' The problem is, of course, that 'justice' itself is elusive, impossible to define; all attempts at it are themselves constantly to be deconstructed, their self-contradictions to be exposed. But here is the difference: it is always deconstructed, as everything else is too, in the name of justice. And justice is 'relation to the other'. In the end (although there is no end to deconstruction) it is the dignity of a person with a claim to justice, someone who has a name, someone who has been called by name, someone who is a 'you', a presence (much like the *du* we meet in Celan's poetry) who calls us. As Derrida himself wrote in *Force of Law*: 'Deconstruction is Justice'.

Of course deconstruction can (and must) be applied to religious language and practice too. Such deconstruction may reveal how religion can disguise the exercise of power. And for many people today (and always) their experience of religious language has been one of a power which silences the smaller disorderly voices of human experience and turns away from the person with a claim on justice. Derrida's deconstruction seeks justice in this religious discourse too. And this, of course, may very well remind us of the prophecy of Amos that we read about earlier in this book, as he deconstructs the religious festivals and language of his contemporaries, the ancient Hebrews:

249

I hate, I despise your feasts,
and I take no delight in your solemn assemblies.
... Take away from me the noise of your songs;
to the melody of your harps I will not listen.
But let justice roll down like waters,
and righteousness like an everflowing stream.

The deconstruction of cult is not a twentieth-century philosophical theory. It is precisely the biblical prophetic tradition about God. We may even be reminded of the words of Jesus himself:

"Woe to you, scribes and Pharisees, hypocrites!
for you tithe mint and dill and cumin,
and have neglected the weightier matters of the law,
justice and mercy and faith." (Matthew 23:23).

This Gospel passage was not a Christian critique of Judaism. It is a prophetic, deconstructive and Derridaean critique of all religion which neglects justice. Likewise Saint Paul, writing to the Corinthians, deconstructs the central ritual assembly of the early Christian church, the Eucharist or Lord's Supper, as he accuses them: when you gather together 'it is not the Lord's supper that you eat', because you humiliate the poor and leave them hungry; in fact 'you are eating and drinking damnation on yourselves' (1 Corinthians 11).

Because of his ceaseless and determined deconstruction of all language, and because for most of his life he never seemed to be *religious* or *a believer* – and I put those words in italics because Derrida would do so, as a distancing sign that these very words are themselves in need of deconstruction – those who knew him and knew his writing believed he was an atheist. Or perhaps I should say *atheist*. Derrida goes further, especially in the last few years of his life. He begins to talk about waiting for a Messiah, though warning that any actual

250

account of any actual Messiah would have to be deconstructed. But the *encounter* with a Messiah is an encounter with justice and peace, and so is beyond deconstruction. He begins to talk about faith and trust – any kind of society, and any kind of human communication, must be built on trust and faith in one another: "You cannot address the other, speak to the other, without an act of faith, without testimony." And finally he says this (*Circumfession*, 154-5):

> That's what my readers won't have known about me, the comma of my breathing henceforward, without continuity but without a break, the changed time of my writing, graphic writing, through having lost its interrupted verticality, almost with every letter, to be bound better and better but be read less and less well over almost twenty years, like my religion about which nobody understands anything any more than does my mother, who asked other people a while ago, not daring to talk to me about it, if I still believed in God ... But she must have known that the constancy of God in my life is called by other names, so that I quite rightly pass for an atheist, the omnipresence to me of what I call God in my absolved, absolutely private language being neither that of an eyewitness nor that of a voice doing anything other than talking to me without saying anything, nor a transcendent law or an immanent *schechina*, that feminine figure of a Yahweh who remains so strange and so familiar to me.

Ultimately, for Derrida, though he says he 'quite rightly passes for an atheist', it is legitimate to use the word 'God' of the undeconstructible justice, of the 'coming' that he says he is waiting for, of the silence or the nothing. Of course, this God is beyond all statements, beyond all religion, because every statement and every religion can be deconstructed. But the very possibility of deconstruction implies something unspoken and indescribable, something beyond, which cannot be deconstructed:

> the great pardon which has not yet happened ... which is why I am addressing myself here to God, the only one I take as a witness, without yet knowing what these sublime words mean, and this grammar, and *to*, and *witness*, and *God*, and *take*, take God, and yet not only do I pray, as I have never stopped doing all my life, and pray to him ...

What is he talking about? He doesn't know what these words – *to, witness, God, take* – mean. Yet God is his witness, even if he doesn't know what he means by the word. He prays to this God, without knowing what the word *God* means. While everything, everything conceivable, may be deconstructed, dissected, exposed, in the end there is the unspeakable, which is what empowers him to do all this deconstructing, and which itself (because it is not a construct, nor a text, nor an idea, nor a cultural artefact, nor even a belief) is beyond deconstruction. Deconstruction is not a twentieth-century invention which religious people need to feel threatened by – even deconstruction of the word 'God'. It is, if anything, a biblical and prophetic invention which believers need. It is part of the old Judaeo-Christian urge to demolish the idols, refusing to worship anything, and when we worship nothing, then (as Derrida nearly said) we may know that God has come and made his dwelling.

BIBLIOGRAPHY.

Augustine, *Confessiones*, in J. P. Migne (ed.) *Patrologia Latina* 32 (Paris, 1841), 660-868 [also in translation by Henry Chadwick, *Saint Augustine Confessions* (Oxford, 1991).

Bentley Hart, David, *Atheist Delusions: The Christian Revolution and its Fashionable Enemies* (New Haven, 2009).

Bottomore, T. B., *Early Writings: Marx* (London, 1975).

Brenner, William, 'D. Z. Philips and Classical Theism', *New Blackfriars* 90 (2008), 17-37

Bullivant, Stephen, 'We Confess that we are Atheists', *New Blackfriars* 101 (2020), 120-34.

Burrell, David B., *Aquinas, God and Action* (London, 1979).

Burrell, David B., 'Distinguishing God from the World', in Brian Davies (ed.), *Language, Meaning and God* (London, 1987), 75-91.

Celan, Paul, *Selected Poems*, Michael Hamburger (ed.) (London, 1996).

Colledge, Edmund and McGinn, Bernard (eds.), *Meister Eckhart: The Essential Sermons, Commentaries, Treatises and Defense* (Mahwah, NJ, 1981).

Dallie, Stephanie (ed.), *Myths from Mesopotamia: Creation, The Flood, Gilgamesh and Others* (Oxford, 1989).

Davies, Brian, 'Classical Theism and the Doctrine of Divine Simplicity', in Brian Davies (ed.), *Language, Meaning and God: Essays in Honour of Herbert McCabe OP* (London, 1987), 51-74.

Davies, Brian, 'Aquinas on what God is not', *Revue Internationale de Philosophie*, 52 (1998), 207-25.

Dawkins, Richard, *The God Delusion* (London, 2006).

De Botton, Alain, *Religion for Atheists* (London, 2012).

Derrida, Jacques, with Geoffrey Bennington, *Jacques Derrida* (including Bennington, *Derridabase* and Derrida *Circumfession: fifty-nine periods and periphrases written in a sort of internal margin, between Geoffrey Bennington's book and work in preparation (January 1989-April 1990)* (Chicago, 1993).

Derrida, Jacques, *The Work of Mourning*, Pascale-Anne Brault and Michael Naas (eds.), (Chicago, 2001).

De Vaux, Roland, 'Tirzah', in D. W. Thomas (ed.), *Archaeology and Old Testament* Study (Oxford, 1967).

Ellis, Marc H., *Toward a Jewish Theology of Liberation* (London, 1988).

Felstiner, John, *Paul Celan: Poet, Survivor, Jew* (New Haven and London, 1995).

Fokin, Alexey, 'Elements of apophatic theology in the writings of Marius Victorinus', *Silenzio e parola nella Patristica, XXXIX incontro de studiosi dell'antichità cristiana* (Rome, 2012), 509-519.

Harbour, Daniel, *An Intelligent Person's Guide to Atheism* (London, 2001).

Hitchens, Christopher, *God is Not Great: The Case Against Religion* (London, 2007) (later published in USA as *God is Not Great: How Religion Poisons Everything*).

Hurtado, Larry W., *Destroyer of the Gods: Early Christian Distinctiveness in the Roman World* (Waco, 2016).

Karrer, Otto (ed.), *Meister Eckhart Speaks* (New York, 1956)

Kenny, Anthony, *The Five Ways* (London, 1969).

Kenny, Anthony, *The Unknown God* (London, 2004).

Kerr, Fergus, *Theology after Wittgenstein* (Oxford, 1986).

Kerr, Fergus, *After Aquinas* (Oxford, 2002).

Lash, Nicholas, *Holiness, Speech and Silence: Reflections on the Question of God* (Aldershot, 2004).

Lash, Nicholas, *Seeing in the Dark: University Sermons* (London, 2005).

Luibheid, Colm (ed. and trans.), *Pseudo-Dionysius: the Complete Works* (London, 1987).

McCabe, Herbert, *Knowing and Naming God*, vol. 3 of *St Thomas Aquinas, Summa Theologiae*, (series editor Thomas Gilby (London and New York, 1964).

McCabe, Herbert, *God Matters* (London, 1987).

McCabe, Herbert, *God Still Matters*, ed. Brian Davies (London, 2002),

McCabe, Herbert, *On Aquinas*, ed Brian Davies (London, 2008).

McGinn, Bernard (ed.), *Meister Eckhart: Teacher and Preacher* (Mahwah NJ, 1986).

McLauchlan, Richard, *Saturday's Silence: R. S. Thomas and Paschal Reading* (Cardiff, 2016).

Márkus, Gilbert, 'Pelagianism and the "Common Celtic Church"', *Innes Review* 56 (2005), 165-213.

Miranda, José Porfirio, *Marx and the Bible: a critique of the Philosophy of Repression* (London, 1977).

Moore, Gareth, 'God as Nothing', unpublished S.T.L. thesis, Blackfriars, Oxford (1984).

Moore, Gareth, *Believing in God: A Philosophical Essay* (Edinburgh, 1988).

Norris, Christopher, *Derrida* (London, 1987; Fontana Modern Masters series).

Pieper, Josef, *The Silence of St Thomas* (London, 1957).

Pseudo-Dionysius: *Pseudo-Dionysius: The Complete Works*, trans. Colm Luibheid (London, 1987).

Rees, B. R., *The Letters of Pelagius and his Followers* (Woodbridge, 1991).

255

Sandars, N. K. (ed.), *The Epic of Gilgamesh* (London, 1972).

Steiner, George, *Real Presences* (London, 1989).

Stenger, Victor, *God: The Failed Hypothesis* (Buffalo NY, 2007).

Thomas, R. S., *Mass for Hard Times* (Newcastle, 1992).

Thomas, R. S., *Collected Poems: 1945-1990* (London, 1993).

Tugwell, Simon (ed.), *Albert and Thomas: Selected Writings* (London, 1988).

Turner, Denys, *The Darkness of God: negativity in Christian mysticism* (Cambridge, 1995).

Turner, Denys, 'Marxism, liberation theology and the way of negation', in Christopher Rowland (ed.), *The Cambridge Companion to Liberation Theology* (Cambridge, 2007), 229-47.

Von Rad, Gerhard, 'Some Aspects of the Old Testament World View', in *The Problem of the Hexateuch and Other Essays*, trans. E.W. Truman Dicken (New York, 1966).

Walshe, M. O'C. (ed.), *Meister Eckhart: Sermons and Treatises*, three volumes (Longmead, Dorset, 1987).

Wittgenstein, Ludwig, *Tratatus Logico-Philosophicus* (London, 1961).

Wittgenstein, Ludwig, *Philosophical Investigations* (Oxford, 1963).

Wittgenstein, Ludwig, *Lectures and Conversations on Aesthetics, Psychology & Religious Belief*, ed. Cyril Barrett (Oxford, 1966).

Wittgenstein, Ludwig, *Culture and Value* (second edition: Oxford, 1980).

Wittgenstein, Ludwig, *Zettel* (second edition: Oxford, 1981).